Bequest Of Wings A Family S Pleasures With Books

"Bequest of Wings"

The Duffs are four: mother, father,
Steven and Deirdre. Their books are legion, and in presenting the picture of
their life together Annis Duff has written
a wise and witty dissertation on the bringing up of children. She is concerned with
living and *being*. She writes about books,
yes—but she shows how books make a
center of interest for themselves, in their
words, ideas, characters, philosophy, fun,
nonsense, beauty, and then point the way
to so many other arts music, painting,
dancing, conversation, the whole art of
living in this world

"Bequest of Wings"

A FAMILY'S PLEASURES WITH BOOKS

Annis Duff

He ate and drank the precious words,
His spirit grew robust,
He knew no more that he was poor,
Or that his frame was dust.
He danced along the dingy ways,
And this bequest of wings
Was but a book. What liberty
A loosened spirit brings!

—*Emily Dickinson*

NEW YORK

The Viking Press

1944

FIRST PUBLISHED APRIL 1944
SECOND PRINTING JUNE 1944

TO

MY GOOD COMPANIONS,

RAMSAY, DEIRDRE, and STEVEN DUFF

Author's Note

To avoid confusion in the reader's mind as to the number and ages of the children whose doings are described in these pages, it may be well to explain that there are two, aged respectively ten and four years. Various chapters were written at various points in their careers, which accounts for some apparent discrepancies, and also, these children, like most, have a habit of advancing their ages with disconcerting rapidity.

A. D.

Acknowledgments

For the use of copyright poems and prose passages, the author makes grateful acknowledgment to the following:

The Bobbs-Merrill Company for the quotation from *The Unexpected Years* by Laurence Housman, Copyright 1936. Used by special permission of the Publishers.

Brandt & Brandt, Agents, for Edna St Vincent Millay's "Grown-up" from *A Few Figs from Thistles,* published by Harper & Brothers. Copyright, 1918, 1919, 1922, by Edna St. Vincent Millay.

Wm. Collins Sons & Co, Ltd. for a passage from Lawrence Alma-Tadema's introduction to *Mother Goose Nursery Rhymes.*

E. P. Dutton & Co, Inc for a passage from *Bright Morning* by Charlie May Simon.

Harper & Brothers for passages from *On the Banks of Plum Creek, By the Shores of Silver Lake, The Long Winter,* and *The Little Town on the Prairie,* all by Laura Ingalls Wilder, reprinted by special arrangement with the Publishers.

Mrs. William B. Heelis of Sawrey, Westmoreland, England, for passages from the books of Beatrix Potter, published by Frederick Warne & Co., Ltd.

Holiday House, Inc for a passage from *Boomba Lives in Africa* by Caroline Singer and LeRoy Baldridge.

Henry Holt and Company for "Yonder See the Morning Blink," Number XI in *Last Poems* by A. E. Housman; and for eight lines from "Someone" by Walter de la Mare.

Houghton Mifflin Company for a paragraph from Horace Scudder's *Childhood in Literature and Art;* and for the first stanza of "Sir Robin," by Lucy Larcom.

Alfred A. Knopf, Inc. for a passage from Walter de la Mare's "The Three Mulla-Mulgars."

Little, Brown & Company for Emily Dickinson's "He ate and drank the precious words" from *The Poems of Emily Dickinson,* edited by Martha

Dickinson Bianchi and Alfred Leete Hampson; for two stanzas of "Alice's Supper" from *Tirra Lirra* by Laura E. Richards, and for the list of things the penguin took into the ice-box, from *Mr. Popper's Penguins* by Florence and Richard Atwater.

Longmans, Green and Co., Inc. for eight lines from "Farewell" by Walter de la Mare.

The Macmillan Company for two passages from *Away Goes Sally* by Elizabeth Coatsworth.

Alida Monro and the Poetry Bookshop for two poems by Harold Monro, "Milk for the Cat" and "Overheard on a Saltmarsh," published by Chatto & Windus.

T. Sturge Moore and Macmillan & Co., Ltd. for the first stanza of "Beautiful Meals" by T. Sturge Moore.

Charles Scribner's Sons for "At the Seaside" and "The Cow" from *A Child's Garden of Verses* by Robert Louis Stevenson.

The Society of Authors, as literary representative of the Trustees of the estate of the late A. E. Housman, and Jonathan Cape, Ltd., for "Yonder See the Morning Blink," Number XI in *Last Poems* by A. E. Housman.

Frederick A. Stokes Company for the poems "Ned" and "Poetry" by Eleanor Farjeon from *Sing for Your Supper*.

The Viking Press, Inc. for "All Mothers Speak to Mary" from *The Long Christmas* by Ruth Sawyer, Copyright 1941, for two passages from *Dobry* by Monica Shannon, Copyright 1934; for three passages from *The Hill of Little Miracles* by Valenti Angelo, Copyright 1942; for two passages from *Tag-Along Tooloo* by Frances Clarke Sayers, Copyright 1941, for two passages from *The Three Policemen* by William Pène du Bois, Copyright 1938

Diligent search has failed to reveal the copyright owner of the Celtic rune, "The Blessing of the Kindling," which appears in Chapter XV. For this, and for any other copyright material which may by inadvertence have been included without specific permission having been given, the author begs indulgence and offers sincere thanks.

The author wishes to record here her affectionate thanks for many loving kindnesses shown by Bertha E. Mahony and Beulah Folmsbee of *The Horn Book Magazine*; specifically, for permission to reprint Chapters II, V, VI, and IX, which appeared in *The Horn Book Magazine*, thanks are given.

For generous and friendly services of divers kinds, the author extends warm thanks to friends and kindred who have made the writing of this book a pure delight. Particularly to Jean Kastrup, secretary in excelsis; to Mildred Ostvold, guide, critic, and friend; and to Jean McElroy, a "conditioned listener" whose capacity for enjoyment knows no peer, the author acknowledges a boundless debt of gratitude.

Contents

CONTENTS

"Bequest of Wings"

CHAPTER ONE

"The Fair Rewards"

THIS is the simple tale of our family's pleasures with books; of how we've grown together in sharing our fun with them; and of how two of us have found the way to being better parents through the use of them.

It is probably just as well that there is no specified training for parenthood beyond just living. There is no job in the world where rules are so likely to be a delusion and a snare. For every child is different from every other child in potentialities, disposition and temperament, and needs his own special kind of parents. We have discovered through ten checkered years of parenthood—not all beer and skittles by any means—that what you need most of all in developing the *whole child,* is to be as nearly as possible a whole person, and to be able to use all of yourself in your education and enjoyment of your children. We have crashed against the barriers of our own limitations time and again, as all parents do. But giving the very best of ourselves always —subject, of course, to the inevitable hinderings of fatigue and the inadequacy of twenty-four hours for any day's affairs—has proved an investment that yields rich dividends in fun and companionship, and the satisfaction of watching sturdy growth.

The dictionary defines education as the "cultivation and development of the various physical, intellectual, aesthetic, moral and social faculties; instruction and discipline." The responsibility for all of this is laid on the parents. Nature, in effect, simply hands over a parcel of assorted energies, and says, "Here, see what you can do with this." And all that two blissful and bewildered people have in the way of preparation for the job is what they have been able to learn from life, up to that point, and what they go on learning as they grow up with their children. We were as awkward a pair of parents as ever launched blithely on a career of exploring and developing human personality. But we knew without much discussion what our hope was for our children—that they should grow fully and robustly and merrily into a fine abundant life, rich with all the things that had brought so much joy to us as individuals, and to our relationships as friends. We had no clear idea of how we should show them the way, except that we must give them as much of ourselves as we possibly could.

It fell to my lot, in a fashion, to set the key with our first baby. As happens in most families, most of her waking hours were spent with me; and that was how books came to play so large a part in our family life. For books were the one thing I really knew about. Ever since my early high-school days, work with books and children was what I most wanted to do. And that was because in my own childhood, as far back as I could remember, books had shed a glow of delight on everything I did. Here, then, was an ex-librarian and bookseller, using the thing she knew best, as a sort of spring-board into all the other things she knew her firstborn must learn.

It wasn't at all a studied method. I do not remember that I was ever very much aware of how extensive and diverse a use I was making of books. All that mattered was that there was security, and the most wonderful fun, in knowing rhymes and poems and little stories that always seemed to be just right for every mood and every stage of our baby's understanding. As we moved along through the first and second and third years, finding fresh delight every day in the books we'd begun to read together, as well as the old poems and stories that came as spontaneously as if I were making them up as I went along, I knew I'd stumbled on something that was going to mean a great deal to our family. For the three of us together were having a royally good time with things that were really a part of us, things that belong to every generation of parents and children and are of the very tissue of human living. The years between have proved that I was right. Books have been for us a real "bequest of wings."

I think there has never been any tendency with us to substitute books for life. The two have been reciprocal in their importance. For the real value of a satisfactory read-ing life is that it gives you the key to other minds in all ages. You find a keener pleasure in all that lies about you be-cause of knowing how other human creatures have felt about it, and the unfamiliar comes close and real because you see it through eyes as eager and curious as your own. Real books grow out of active desire to give permanence to some experience, spiritual or imaginative or intellectual or social. These are the books that embody the real history and spirit of mankind because they have life. Books as far apart in character as *War and Peace* and *Alice in Wonderland* have this in common, that they release new energies in the minds that absorb them. This is the reason why there is no sterility in our family reading—we go on together from one fascinating view of life to another, and because we care more for living than for having, I think we tend to use books as a means of coming closer in understanding and sympathy to the rest of the human family. This gives us a sort of stability, very comforting, especially now when it is almost impossible to avoid questioning beliefs and values traditionally held dependable.

Children need security and a sense of permanence. While they are young and dependent, they find them in the homely round of family life and in the steadfast love of parents who believe in them. But they must be prepared from their very earliest days to stand on their own feet; and we believe that letting them share as far as they can all the resources that the "constant mind of man" has provided will give them confidence in the value of the human race, and in their own positive responsibility and ableness for preserving what is best in it.

Now lest anyone should suppose that we began our family's "literary" career with a sense of solemn duty and a stern determination to make life real and earnest, I must state emphatically that our purpose in using books so lavishly with our young has been, so far as they are concerned, at any rate, purely hedonistic. We do it for fun. Anything else is a by-product. The by-products have been excellent and varied, and that is a tremendous slice of luck.

It must not be thought, either, that my having been a "professional bookwoman" gave me any special advantage other than that it had kept me in touch with what was being published for children. Any mother who herself loves books can make herself familiar with what is available for her children.

People have often said to us, "How does it happen that your children know so many books? Mine have never asked for them." It does not just "happen"; children seldom do *ask* for books, as an initial stage in learning to love them. Reading, for young children, is rarely a pleasure in isolation, but comes through shared pleasure and constant discerning exposure to books so that they fall naturally into the category of pleasant necessities, along with food, sleep, music and all out-of-doors. If the parents really want a child to have the fun of being a great reader, or if the child feels any need of it at all, I am fairly confident that it can be managed with a little intelligent effort. The important thing to remember, is that "you can lead a horse to water but you cannot make him drink." We have the greatest respect for a child's independence in his choice and judgment of books, and that may be one reason why (apart from inherited love of reading) our children have fallen so readily into the family habit.

We have given just as much consideration to the choice of books for them as for any grown-ups. We are genuinely interested in their interests; we know their current tastes; and we know how much their experience of life has equipped them to understand and enjoy. No child in this family has ever been pressed to read or look at a book that he (or she) has no inclination for. We say, "This books looks like good fun," or "Here's something you might enjoy"; and occasionally "I wish you'd have a look at this and tell me what you think of it." Our two bairns hear their parents recommending books to each other in just that fashion, they know that there is no attempt to coerce or impose. It is sometimes difficult not to be more emphatic with our ten-year-old daughter when we have found a real prize. But she has her own tempo, and does not like to be pushed; she will usually arrive at reading a good book, perhaps months after we have mentioned it, whereas if we had been too persistent she might have asserted her independence by avoiding it like the plague.

When, on the other hand, she explodes "Oh, Mum and Duff, you've just *got* to read this book!" we take it as a compliment, usually finding that what she has recommended is absolutely essential to our happiness! And when we go up to bed, and find that a thoughtful four-year-old has put *Little Black Sambo* on my pillow, and *The Little House* on his father's, we feel that there simply is nothing in the world quite so much fun as living with our own children!

When we are asked how to find the right books for children, I am a little puzzled to know what to say, for the usefulness of any advice depends on how much, if anything, the individual parent knows of children's books to begin with, and at what stage of a child's development the program is to be taken up: whether he is a brand-new person, or has already had some exposure to books, and what the nature of such exposure has been. But the public library of almost any town is likely to be a steady and reliable source of information, and there are many good books on childrens' reading to be had, with extensive lists of titles. *Realms of Gold,* with its supplement *Five Years of Children's Books* are my great favorites, and they are a liberal education especially for the parents who are "starting from scratch." Then there is *The Horn Book,* a magazine concerned with "books and reading for young people" which provides sound information about the new books for children of all ages, and frequent authoritative articles on the "standard" ones. Many splendid and stimulating books about reading with children have appeared during the last few years, and these will make their appeal as the parent's knowledge grows and enthusiasm warms.

But this is only the beginning. The parent who is really in earnest about finding out what is for children to read and how to bring book and child together, will need to develop some sort of judgment of his own. The same standards that determine what is or is not a good book for a grown-up can be applied to books for children as well, provided you keep in mind always that there is no value for any child in a thing for which *nothing in his experience* has given him the key. A grown-up who has a nice taste in books will find

that with a little adjustment in his point of view he can
acquire skill at "nosing out" good books for a child that he
is in tune with. Sensitiveness to the child's response will
keep him clear of disastrous errors in judgment, and a certain flexibility and a wholesome ingredient of humility,
combined with genuine interest in and enjoyment of what
the child enjoys, will soon show him how to go about his
pleasant job with some degree of sureness.

Time after time I go back to a paragraph from Horace
Scudder's *Childhood in Literature and Art* that I found
many years ago. It seemed then, as it seems now, a perfect
summing up of what parents ought to know about how to
choose books for their children:

"I think the solution of the problem that vexes us will be
found not so much in the writing of good books for children, as
in the wise choice of those parts of the world's literature which
contain an appeal to the child's nature and understanding. It
is not so much the books written expressly for children, so much
as it is the books written out of minds that have not lost their
childhood that will form the body of literature which shall be
classic for the young."

That disposes of all the books that are written *for* children
because the author thinks a book for a child does not require
as muscular thinking or as fine craft as a book for a grown-up.
It includes all the honest books, that are written with knowledge, insight, humor and imagination, and put together with
the skill and artistry that respect for language and style demand. These are the books that come to live in the family li-

brary, especially when the need for careful spending dictates fastidious choosing. *Winnie-the-Pooh* and *The Wind in the Willows* can rub shoulders with *The Crock of Gold* and the *Plays of William Shakespeare,* without incongruity; for they are made of the same permanent stuff, laughter and pain, hunger and satisfaction, and an infinite love of all the bittersweet ingredients of human life. These are the books that I mean when I speak of coming closer in sympathy and understanding, through reading, to the whole of the human family. For "those parts of the world's literature that contain an appeal to the child's nature and understanding" have the same truth to life as the "great books" that he will grow up to. They present on his own level, and in a way that gives him pleasure, the "experience spiritual or imaginative or intellectual or social" that one generation records for the delight and enrichment of all succeeding generations. Through the power that they have over him *because he does enjoy them,* he begins to learn something of respect for human personality, enjoyment of its special flavor, and tolerance of what he does not understand in it. They open doors into more aspects of heaven and earth than his infant philosophy has dreamed of, and through them he begins to learn what Man really is.

All children read some books of doubtful pedigree, just as their parents do; and so they should if only not to fall into the grievous error of intellectual pride. But children who have a solid foundation of real literature develop a richness of mental and spiritual texture that not only enhances their charm as peerless companions but increases their value as Real People. We have watched the process in our ten-year-old daughter with wonder and delight, and our man-child, now a stalwart four-year-old, shows promise of a totally different but equally enthralling growth into the things we most want him to have and to be.

"What liberty a loosened spirit brings!"

CHAPTER TWO

A Family Affair

. . . these family readings formed so satisfying a bond between elder and younger that I can hardly think of family
life without it; and I marvel when I hear of families in
whose upbringing it has had no place.—*Laurence Housman, at the age of seventy, in "The Unexpected Years."* [1]

I wonder what families do that don't read books together?
It's like not knowing each other's friends.—*A Young Person, aged eight.*

IT was a happy accident, coming out of a desire to do things
together, rather than from a conscious effort to cultivate
a bookish habit of mind in our small companion, that
launched us, when she was only half-past one, into a career
of reading *en famille.* We had always, from the day she was
hatched, spoken poetry to her, and said or sung nursery
rhymes—these things make good "conversation" for a
solemn small person who lies on a bath-table and listens
with gratifying attention. So what could be more natural,
when she had reached the creeping stage, than that she
should come close to listen when one read to the other?

It seemed unkind to talk over her head always, so one day,

[1] Bobbs-Merrill, 1937

23

after we had been singing out of *The Baby's Opera,* I took her on my knee and showed her Walter Crane's nice pictures while I spoke the rhymes. It was not a sensational success; she wriggled and fidgeted, and after a while slid down and went off to her own work. But it was not very long before she brought books, climbed upon the Olympian knee, and listened to verses while the pages were turned over slowly to show the pictures. When such *tête-à-têtes* became more and more frequent, the third member of the family tended to drift into the picture; and presently the bedtime ceremonies included what we have now learned to call a "reading period."

One by one the small listener's own books, some left over from the parents' babyhood, and some the pristine purchases of discerning relatives, came into use. It was a revelation to find what excitement and pleasure popped out from the pages, and the education of two young parents began in real earnest. That even very tiny children have definite interests became manifest at once; how absurdly and delightfully funny it was to discover that whereas a two-year-old girl baby had loved pictures of other babies, and furry animals, and all soft and pretty things, a two-year-old gentleman loves cars and trains and boats, and has a passion for wheels. A grown-up will exhibit a facile tact in commenting on books you suggest; a small child, never. So there is endless fun in discovering what books and pictures will appeal to your young hopeful, and the search for suitable material takes you into fresh woods and pastures new every time you go into a library or a bookshop.

That the standard of text, pictures, and general quality in books for little children must be high goes without saying. I believe that good taste, if it is not actually instinctive in "new people," can be developed with great sureness; and there can be no possible excuse for accepting anything other than the best that is to be had. I question the validity of the often-heard complaint that there are so few good books for little children. It must be remembered that a great number of books at one time tend to confuse; small people like to look at the same ones over and over again, which is a further reason for choosing books that will wear well not only physically but artistically as well. A third reason for demanding a high standard of quality is that no parent who is not totally insensitive, or self-sacrificing to the point of fatuity, could endure to look at any of the rubbishy, falsely-conceived books of a purely commercial origin often enough to satisfy the demands of an eager child. A book, to be good enough for a little child, must have qualities that make it acceptable to an intelligent adult. In only a very few instances in our own experience has it happened that one child or the other has shown great interest in a book that was definitely uninteresting to the parents; and then it was doubtless that the child saw something appealing that we, with our clouded grown-up eyes, could not see.

The striking characteristic of the pictures in the really good books that are used first of all is that they show with intensified clarity, and with beauty, vitality, humor and charm, the things that a child is likely to see in everyday experience. They invest these ordinary things with the brightness of the artist's vision. So a child who has lived with the lambs in *The Christ Child* will not see a live lamb merely as a woolly object in a meadow; he will see a very special kind of lamb that shares something of beauty and holiness. These fine picture books—and they are legion—deserve to be savored, and this is where the parents, as much as the little child, find deep and satisfying pleasure in studying them together often and slowly.

The sharing of beauty can never begin too early, and the child who from his baby years has been helped to see beauty "will love all that is beautiful, and hate all that is ugly, long before he knows the reason why." There need be nothing studied or stuffy about cultivating a child's sense of visual beauty through books; Leslie Brooke's drawings of pigs are just as beautiful, in their droll way, as the Petershams' exquisitely tender drawings of the lambs. The quality of enjoyment varies with the mood of the pictures, and it is the enjoyment of beauty that perpetuates it. Here, then, is the secret of the successful use of picture books in family reading: to choose what is suitable for the mood of the moment, and to enter wholeheartedly into the child's delight in what evokes his response.

For a good many months, the reading that goes along with the pictures is mostly, one supposes, a sound pleasant in itself, and enhanced by association with visual pleasure. It establishes the habit of listening, and the pleasures that come from reading aloud as a family while "the child is yet a tender thing" shadow forth the increasing delights of being partners in exploring with eagerness and curiosity all the treasures of the mind stored up in books. In the beginning, what one reads is usually familiar from one's own infancy, since jingles and rhymes from Mother Goose, old nursery rhymes and songs, are the natural heritage of the very young. But always when I read them aloud or hear them read, I think of the lady who went into a bookshop to buy gifts for nephews and nieces; after she had been shown a great many books she said, "But these are all old books." Whereupon the bookseller remarked gently, "Yes, Madam, but the children are always new."

Somehow, with every reading, the old verses take on new freshness for the new listeners, and one has a sort of springtime urge to make them more beguiling than they have ever sounded before. To do this it is necessary not only to be able to read beautifully, but to sing sweetly, and one realizes what a vast equipment of accomplishments the ideal parent would require! But one of the jolliest things about reading to little children is that much of what is suitable for them goes naturally into music, which is also their heritage. "Everyone suddenly burst out singing"—and there is no better way than that of teaching people who are learning to talk that there is music in words, and that they therefore should be spoken musically. The meaning and use of words, too, comes most quickly to a child who is read or sung to; he begins early to show a lively interest in new words, picks them up and plays with them, enjoying the "feel" and the sound of his own voice saying them. This is the beginning of delight in the subtleties of language, and leads to a discriminating and accurate use of it.

Soon it is possible to read simple stories, and verses with a longer musical line and deeper feeling than the nursery rhymes, and the quality of writing must always be high. Purity and simplicity of language, directness of thought, vitality of expression and the use of faithful images in what children hear read help them to avoid shabbiness and mediocrity when they begin to choose books for themselves. Our family's reading together became more and more interesting as the field of choice expanded with the expanding mind of the little listener; and not only were we having wonderful fun, but the small person, with that stimulus, was beginning to explore books for herself. Some of the books that we had read were now her own memory's possession, and she delighted to trip us up on a word left out or misplaced, and could "read" to herself, accurately allotting each bit of text to its proper picture—a circumstance that distressed a visiting grandfather, who questioned the wisdom of burdening the little mind with the work of learning to read before its third birthday! All of this was amusing, but the real profit lay in the fact that we now shared a respectable store of real literature.

She began, too, to cultivate the art of the apt quotation. Never shall I forget one dark, quiet winter afternoon, when there was no sound in the house but the whisper of a pencil across paper, and the subdued scufflings of the three-year-old among her toys on the floor. Suddenly from the basement came a small trickling rattle, of coal running down in the bin. The three-year-old looked up with interest, listened for a moment, and then said solemnly, "Down, down, down, like money in a money-box!" From then on her conversation has continued to be studded with quotations. This may seem a trivial thing, to be able to quote tags from books; but there is great intimacy in the quick response to a familiar reference, like Mrs. Miniver's catching of the sympathetic eye across a dinner-table.

Now that there are four of us, we first ones, for the general family reading, have gone back to picture books, some that we have shared before and will always love, and some—like the delightful Polish *Locomotive*, Père Castor's *Allons Vite*, and Lois Lenski's *The Little Train*—that are peculiarly a little boy's. Just now he is learning that books are fun, and therefore precious and to be cared for; and we are trying to show him, through experience, what his sister has already learned: that there are few better ways of finding out about a thing than to look it up in a book—even if the Montgomery Ward Catalogue is the only book you possess with the right kind of picture.

It will be fun for us all to travel again, with our new companion, through the delights of Beatrix Potter and A. A. Milne; we shall rejoice if he loves *The Wind in the Willows* as we do, and spend another blissful summer with *The Wonderful Adventures of Nils*, hoping that he will wait on tiptoe with excitement for each next day's chapter. And perhaps we shall find again, with him, the occasion to discuss the preciousness of all life, when we read how Curdie shot the pigeon, and knew for the first time, when he held it in his hands, "what a pigeon really is." It may be that some of these pleasures that we have shared will not be for him. But he will show us other treasures, and four minds, stimulated by each other, will find both common and separate gifts of pleasure, understanding, beauty, and fun.

So, from the sharing of books in intimate family pleasures with the smallest of bairns, comes, for the family as a unit, stability and kinship of spirit; and for the little child, the opening of doors to much that makes life good, and shows the dignity of the persistent striving of humanity toward the Good Life. So, too, from these early beginnings comes the growth of the mind in perception of "that which cannot be thought about in words, or told or expressed . . . all the secret and quiet world beyond our lives, wind and stars, too, and the sea, and the endless unknown."

CHAPTER THREE

Strictly Practical:

Notes on training children in the proper use of books

IN several excellent reading lists that I have seen lately, books like Leslie Brooke's *Johnny Crow's Garden* and *Oranges and Lemons* were suggested for four- and five-year-olds, instead of for the nursery population whose pleasure, I am sure, was what Mr. Brooke had most in mind when he made those entrancing pictures. This puzzled me until I realized that such a postponement may be advocated not so much because these books are considered too advanced for very small children, as because of their physical value. Books of this kind, beautifully printed, illustrated and bound, are rather a costly item for the average family's book-budget; and since it is generally assumed that there is nothing to be done about a baby's natural tendency to destroy books, parents shy away from giving them such expensive ones. But babies *can* be taught to handle books properly. It is no easier than any other kind of training required by the young. But I do believe that babies derive so much pleasure and profit from friendship with beautiful books that every expense of patience, tact, and time is rewarded

31

many times over. In the first place, there is no "lag" in the development of their natural good taste and love of beautiful things. And in the second place, it is cheaper in the long run to buy a few good books and take care of them, than to buy inferior ones and let the young hopeful develop his "smaller muscles" by tearing them apart. The latter is a process wasteful both of material and of the baby's capacity for learning—just a bad habit, really, for both parent and child. So, knowing from experience that it can be done, I make a plea that children be trained to handle books with care.

This requires a certain foresight and preparation, and, more than anything else, reasonableness. It is not reasonable, for instance, to expect a child to take care of a thing that he does not respect. He does not respect a book if it does not interest him; nor does he respect it if he is allowed to abuse it. So the initial step in teaching him to use books properly should be first, to establish their value as peerless entertainment; and second, to establish and *live up to* the rule that no book shall be wantonly handled. I consider it a thoroughly bad plan to allow a baby to pull apart the *Saturday Evening Post,* and then to expect him to refrain from treating his proper books in similar fashion. Even his very first cloth picture-books should be given respectful treatment if you are really serious in your intention. Consistent practice in the beginning will save much tedious undoing of bad habits later on.

Now I think very few mothers—or fathers either, for there is no reason why the enjoyment of baby-cum-book should be confined to the distaff side—need to be told how to establish the "pleasure value" of books. It will be in the beginning, I think, a shared pleasure:

> ℞ One relaxed baby, bathed, fed, and at peace with the world; one book of jolly colored pictures; an accommodating parental lap, complete with owner who enjoys the book and shows it in face, hands, voice and whole self. These to be combined and taken slowly every evening, with no interruptions allowed.

The very choicest book can be used in this way with no fear of damage. The little companion can help to hold it, and can be shown how to turn the pages. From his very first acquaintance with books he should be helped to treat them kindly. Once, during a talk to a group of mothers, I described the proper handling of a book, and was surprised to discover that not one of them had ever realized that there is a proper way. Here are four good rules:

1. A book, when new, should be opened carefully to limber it up. Working from both covers, a few pages at a time should be laid open and smoothed down gently until you reach the middle. Never open it abruptly and force it back to make it lie flat.

2. A child should be encouraged to read or look at pictures with the book laid flat on an even surface, or to hold it in both hands. This prevents loosening the binding.

3. Pages should be turned from the outer right-hand side. This seems obvious, but most children seem to want to lift from the inside lower corner, thus tearing and bruising the paper.

4. The bookmark habit should be established early. As soon
as children begin to read books that require more than one
sitting, they are likely to lay them open, face down, to
mark the place—a destructive habit often picked up from
their elders. I recommend the plan of providing each new
book with its own marker, attractively decorated, and bear-
ing the names of the book, the donor, and the recipient.
These are fun to make, and pleasant to use.

The life-span of many books is lengthened if they are
given a little preparatory treatment before being handed
over to the owners:

1. Dust jackets are a useful protection, but they have an ir-
ritating habit of slipping off. Fasten them in place with a
few bits of scotch tape, being careful not to stretch them
tightly enough to prevent the book's opening easily. This
will avoid having them torn by an exasperated baby.

2. Thin books with board covers are apt to come apart, especially if the pages are stitched in only one set. It is a good
plan to fix the book firmly into its cover with two broad
strips of adhesive tape, the full length of the page front
and back. Fold the tape sharply, lay one-half along the
inside of the cover, fit the crease firmly into the angle between cover and book proper (the tip of a blunt paper-
knife drawn firmly down the length of the crease will do
this nicely), then lay the other half of the tape along the
first page and smooth it down. A little practice will pro-
duce results that allow the book to open without stiffness.

3. A "back-strap" of adhesive tape prevents light bindings
from wearing and splitting. Care should be taken in apply-
ing it to leave no "bubbled" edges to tempt little fingers to

pull to see what happens. When I found that my small boy
did not care for bandages on his books, I tried coloring
the tape with tempera paint of a shade to match the binding, and shellacking it to prevent the color rubbing off—
very successful.

4. The whole cover may be shellacked if it has a soft surface
that soils too easily. If this causes warping, weight the book
down, as soon as it is thoroughly dry, under a pile of large
books for a day or two.

When children begin to enjoy looking at books by themselves, they can be taught gradually to put them away in
their appointed place. This cultivates a useful habit of
order, and makes it possible for books to live safely in the
child's own room. The "place for everything" will be decided upon according to the habits of each particular child.
Our first little book-collector had her own bookcase from
a very early age, because she was an orderly soul, and
settled readily into the way of using her books only for their
ordained purpose. Duff Secundus is another sort of character, who "chucks things about" with fine abandon, and
has required rather more persistent training. His books,
therefore, have their place on a high chest-of-drawers, available when he wants them, but not too handy as properties
for his play.

There are inevitably casualties among books, if the child
is allowed free enough use of them to develop his own judgment. It is a good plan to arrange that every deliberate act
of destruction shall be followed by its inevitable consequence: the removal of *all* books for a definite period, such

removal, explained without recrimination, being simply a means of impressing the idea that you forfeit the privilege of using things that you enjoy but do not take care of. (It is important never to apply this corrective in cases of sheer accident. Common justice must be respected if the parent expects to be.)

The value of this kind of training, it seems to me, extends far beyond the immediate good habits it fosters. Its effectiveness with even very tiny children of the happy-go-lucky variety was demonstrated in our own case when our small son lacked several months of two years. He had somehow got hold of his sister's library book, and made a pretty thorough job of dismembering it—great fun! The enormity of the offense was brought home to him when he watched all his treasures being removed from their place on the chest-of-drawers. The next morning, very early, we heard him climbing out of bed, saying to himself in pleased anticipation, "He's going to look at a book." The big chair scraped across the floor toward the chest, "He's going to look at many books." A small body heaved itself up into the chair, "He's going to look at MANY books!" Then, in a tone of bitter disappointment and outrage, "Oh, OH! NO BOOKS!" When, after some time, we went into his room, a penitent little figure sat dolefully in bed, and a very small voice said, "He tore the poor book. Can't look at *any* books."

It is not a good play to deprive the little miscreant of his books for very long. A child's sense of time being as it is, he is likely to forget what caused the trouble, and the value of the lesson is lost. But the damaged book should not be given back with the others. I find it a good plan to keep all books in need of mending in a special drawer in my desk. Then, every so often, instead of reading, we sit together at the nursery table and carefully repair all injuries. All kinds of small jobs can be devised to keep the little helper interested, for it is important that he should take as big a share as possible in restoring his books to health and strength. A large flat box contains the necessary materials:

Scotch tape, on a roller with a cutting edge.
Scissors.
Library paste and spreader.
Adhesive tape, 2½ inch width.
Seamed linen tape (2, 3, 4, 5, and 6 leaf) for replacing detached pages.
Tempera paints.
White shellac.
Small shellac brush.

We seldom attempt to mend more than two or three books at one time, so that when we have finished we can make an occasion of welcoming them back into use. We admire "our" handiwork, look at the pictures, read the story or verses, and generally rejoice. Mending days have become less and less frequent during the past year, and the last time a book was torn the owner, lately turned three, was so genuinely distressed that we realized how great a pride he has achieved in keeping his books intact.

Of course there are some books, of particular value and beauty, that are subject to special treatment and care. It is just as reasonable for little children to learn the value of fine editions as it is for grown-ups to cherish certain volumes, keeping them in a place of their own, safe from dust and casual handling. *Ring o' Roses,* for instance, is our small boy's very own book, but it is kept with our other choice picture-books. We look at it almost every day, but always as a sort of special treat. One afternoon I found myself, much to my surprise, ready for expected company long before the appointed time. So, arrayed in my best bib and tucker and discreetly scented with my best perfume, I settled down with my small friend to enjoy Leslie Brooke's summery pictures. "Dumpty Dumpty," Little Bo-Peep and all the rest were greeted with the usual exuberance of pleasure, and then my companion remarked irrelevantly, "Mummy smells nice." Since then his formula has been, "Now should we look at the 'smell-nice' book?" and he thoroughly enjoys the partyish atmosphere that goes with *Ring o' Roses* and other books of that kind. I think they will always be associated in his mind with the pleasant glow of a festive occasion. When he looks at them by himself, hands clean and face shining with soap and pleasure, his treatment is gentle and controlled; for if these books "give nose and eyes a treat," why should he not give them special loving care?

So the second of our two little bibliophiles shows every day the value of persistent and consistent training in the use of books. It has taken time and patience, certainly. But what, that's worth having, does not? And no one who has lived with a book-loving child will dispute the statement that few things are *more* worth having than the freedom of spirit that comes with the companionship of books.

CHAPTER FOUR

"The Man of It"

THERE is no doubt that "maleness of mind" dictated our small boy's choice of books from the very beginning. He arrived, apparently, with foreknowledge of the delights of wheels; they were his first passion. Boats came next and now the two are equal, and more absorbing than anything else.

We were not very well equipped to handle the situation when he began to look at pictures and books. In our young days the literature of mechanical things was pretty much in its infancy, so that we had no remembrance of favorite books to guide us. All I remembered was Stevenson's train poem, "Faster than fairies, faster than witches"; but that was not the practical approach that our young man required. My bookshop experience with factual picture-books about trains, automobiles, ships and so on, had given me rather a poor opinion of the great majority of them, especially the ones for beginners. They seemed too unimaginative, and lacked the stimulating quality that I felt should be there. Most of them were wretchedly illustrated, with bad drawings in poor color, not at all the sort of thing to satisfy an intelligent child.

But it was obvious from the eagerness with which he examined illustrations in magazines that our boy wanted pictures to supplement his familiarity with actual objects. We set out to see what we could find, because we realized that his fascinated interest in things that go was the logical avenue of approach to interest in books. It was pleasant to find that even in the few years that I had been out of touch with what was being done in this field, a great improvement had been made in presenting suitable material for mechanically minded little boys. Real enthusiasm had in many cases taken the place of desire to instruct, and right at the outset we found two books that remain favorites, not just with their owner, but with the whole family.

When he was eleven months old, and not able to talk yet, Lois Lenski's *The Little Train* appeared. A discerning friend gave it to him for Christmas, and from the time we first showed him the pictures, he has loved it with a pure devotion. For a little while the text held no interest for him, quite naturally, but as soon as he began to have a use for speech, he learned from that book the words he needed to talk about what he was most interested in.

When he was two years old, we stopped one afternoon to look at a train as it stood in the station. He surveyed the engine with a proprietary interest, pointing out the sand-dome, the steam-dome, the headlight and the smokestack, the boiler and the driving-wheels. The engineer was leaning out of his cab window, watching and listening with great amusement. "Somebody in your family certainly knows trains!" he remarked. The eight-year-old member of our party explained that the impressive information came out of a book. "It's called *The Little Train*. You'd love it." "I'm sure I would," he replied. "It sounds like quite a book."

And it *is* quite a book. I was not surprised to learn that a crowd of children had had a hand in making it, for it is so full of the little details that a child loves. The pictures are the main thing, very simple and open, and with an engaging blandness in the faces of the people. The text is what some would call uninspired; it is sparse, written in short sentences with no attempt at style. But I think Lois Lenski intended the book primarily for looking; and the brevity of the sentences gives you time to examine the pictures in between. There is no tiresome business of explaining that the Little Train is owned by a railroad company, and that Engineer Small just runs it.

You are simply told that, "Engineer Small has a little train. The engine is black and shiny. He keeps it oiled and polished. Engineer Small is proud of his little train." Then there is a fine picture of the engine showing the salient features, all clearly labeled: the bell and the whistle, sand-dome, steam-dome, smokestack, boiler and driving-wheels. Then you read about where the engine lives, how it gets out onto the track; how it is fed and watered, and how the train is put together. Then off you go on a trip, seeing all the things along the way—farms and farmhouses, cows and horses in the fields, hills and woods and streams, a boy on a fence waving his hand. You watch for signals, go onto a siding to let the Blue Streak Express go by, wait while a

drawbridge stands open to let a sailboat pass underneath;
you roar through a tunnel and finally come into the station
in the city. The story has no dramatic emphasis whatsoever;
it is simply the thread that holds the pictures together, and
the pictures have all the variety, surprise and movement
that the little reader requires. After three years of almost
daily use, *The Little Train* is still interesting and exciting
to the train-lover in our family.

The next book in his collection was the superb Polish
picture-book *Locomotive,* with rhymes by Tuwim and pictures by Lewitt and Him. Here he found a boisterous
humor in drawings that have color and speed, and words
that go galloping along with the rhythm of the train. This
he took much more slowly than the other, studying the
pictures with a sort of puzzled fascination at first, and showing no interest at all in the rhymes. The whole appearance
of the train is different from anything he had seen, and the
point of view shifts much more frequently than in Lois
Lenski's pictures. He evidently had to make himself at home
before he could accept it with full enjoyment. This took
over a year, and it was funny to see how he gradually relaxed his wariness and finally took *Locomotive* completely
to his heart. He quotes less from it than from other familiar
books, because the rhymes have rather complicated rhyth-
mic patterns for little tongues to master. But he listens
with attention when we read it, and he loves the words, fine
sonorous ones, and uses them with gusto.

There are two other delightfully droll rhymed stories
in the same volume, "Grandfather's Turnip" and "The

Birds' Broadcast," but these had no appeal until quite lately, when they have suddenly proved to be a source of much merriment.

The next item in his collection of train books, *Choo-Choo, the Little Switch-Engine,* was not entirely successful. The author, Wallace Wadsworth, has obviously a real affection for trains, and the skeleton of the story is quite good: the adventures of a little switch-engine who dreams of the time when he will grow up to be a great streamliner; his disappointment when he finds that such things do not happen; and the thrilling occasion when he rescues the big passenger train and proves to himself and to the railroad yard men that he is a very prince of switch-engines. But such material, to be effective, has to be handled with a greater deftness than the book shows. There is far too much text, both confusing and tiring for a little boy. The pictures are in the main well, though not imaginatively, drawn, but they are crowded in among the print on pages too small for them, and the color is harsh and badly balanced, so that the whole book has an unattractive cheapness about it. I cannot say that it has been entirely without appeal; love is blind, and *Choo-Choo* is a book about a train, with lots and lots of pictures of trains, which alone secured it a definite place in our young hopeful's affections. But its binding has a look of newness that betrays its failings. *The Little Train* and *Locomotive,* limp, shabby and much mended, show the results of a little boy's constant and loving use of them.

I had wondered for a while if investing a mechanical object with a human personality was not an altogether bad

thing. I have come to the conclusion that it is not necessarily
fatal, just very dangerous. *Choo-Choo, the Little Switch-
Engine* overdoes the "human hopes and fears" element,
and falls rather flat; whereas, in Virginia Lee Burton's *Choo-
Choo, the Story of a Little Engine Who Ran Away,* the device is used with a lighter touch, just enough to engage the
sympathies of little boys who know what it is to want to
run away. Miss Burton knows the value of economy in telling a story to a small child, and lets the pictures do most
of the work. They are fine pictures with sweeping boldness,
rhythm, speed and drollery, very much to the taste of our
young man when he was three years old, and increasingly
delightful to him now that he is four. His little English
lead train men, who used always to be called Engineer
Small, Fireman Shorty and Conductor Little, are now sometimes called Archibald, Oley and Jim, and the tender of his
smaller train has developed a playful habit of toppling off
a bridge onto a coal-barge below. It begins to look as if
Choo-Choo were creeping up into a class with *The Little
Train* and *Locomotive.*

Two of our most favorite family train books are English
ones, called simply *Trains* and *Our Trains.* These are large
paper picture books with colored representations, almost
photographic in their accuracy, of various British locomo-
tives. Their special importance, apart from their owner's
rapturous interest in them, is that they have been the means
of sharing with him some of the pleasures of our pre-war
summers in Britain. Our daughter, who had made two

trans-Atlantic voyages before she was six, feels very acutely
the fact that the three of us have had momentous adventures of a kind that the war has prevented his having. That
is her one personal quarrel with circumstances, that he will
have no little boy memories of exploring the countryside of
Dorset and poking into all the fascinating corners of Edinburgh. He is too little to enjoy descriptions of places he
has never seen, but trains are another matter. However
curious the shape of a locomotive, and however unfamiliar
the names of the cars it hauls, he feels the attraction. Realiz-
ing this, she draws on all her resources of memory, to invest
the pictures of British trains with a special, personal significance. Fortunately she was much in the company of a grandfather who enjoys few things more than a visit to a railroad,
and she has seen or traveled in many of the famous trains
shown in these books, which gives her great prestige in her
brother's eyes. Almost every picture now has its own story,
and she never tires of telling, nor he of hearing, about the
Flying Scotsman that carried us from London to Edinburgh;
about the Royal Scot that picked up water from a tank
between the tracks while it was going at full speed; or about
the tremendous goods train that went thundering across
the Forth Bridge while we watched from below. The Coronation Scot is the favorite of us all, and our boy begs again
and again for the story of how Mummy, arriving at King's
Cross in London, with only sixteen minutes to make the
connection with the Salisbury train at Waterloo, neverthe-
less "dashed up the platform to stroke the nose of the

Coronation Scot, and it was so clean that her fresh white glove didn't even get a smudge on it!" An awed little voice always asks, "Really, didn't it?"

We love to hear him telling himself that his long wooden train is a "mixed goods train" or "the fish train coming full speed from Aberdeen to London." When travel across the Atlantic is once again a pleasure instead of an ordeal by suspense, there will be one traveler fully "conditioned" to enjoy the major delights of the British Isles.

One or two other train books have a steady if somewhat milder appeal. *The Little Engine That Could* is lots of fun for bedtime telling and incidentally provides the crafty parent with two excellent persuasive devices for difficult moments: a flagging appetite can be stimulated by the suggestion that the "wholesome food" had to be brought by some little engine; and the persistence of the little engine is a fine example to small boys who give up too easily. But this has nothing to do with the real fun of the story.

Lois Donaldson's *Smoky, the Lively Locomotive* is a pleasant, rather unoriginal tale, reminiscent of *The Little Engine That Could* but told with more imaginative detail. The illustrations by Wilhelm Schultz are the real charm of the book, lovely drawings in attractive soft colors, with all sorts of delightful, unexpected details that reflect an affectionate familiarity with the German countryside. The train moves through all the pictures with a persistence most engaging to a small boy, but he cannot escape the appeal of the real beauty in the background, and so he gets a taste of what trains are really for, to take you on wonderful trips to new and exciting places.

During our small boy's second summer on our Georgian Bay island, when he was eighteen months old, the sea-faring blood of his ancestors began to beat strongly in his veins. His very first word was "boat," and we heard it from morning till night. The sight and sound of boats sent him into spasms of joy, and when we had come back in the autumn to our land-locked life, something had to be done to satisfy his longing for water-craft. The two books we found then were fortunately exactly what he wanted, for we have never come across anything since that quite comes up to them. The first was Lois Lenski's *The Little Sail Boat,* done in the same manner as *The Little Train.* Captain Small goes off with a lunch-basket and his small dog Tinker, for a day's fishing in his little sail boat; and somehow you catch an agreeable holiday feeling from it. There is no embroidery in the text; but necessary sailing terms are used correctly and explained simply, and the pictures bring it all to life. There is some subtle quality of imagination in Lois Lenski's books that our lad is susceptible to: he listened to the story and looked at the pictures with an expression of complete bliss before he was two years old, and now, on any indoor day he is likely to collect a small basket, a toy dog, a walking stick for a fishing-rod, and go happily sailing away in an arm-chair to perform with scrupulous exactness and complete satisfaction all the little doings of Captain Small's day.

The second boat book achieved its success by sheer force of personality. *Little Toot,* the New York harbor tug-boat, *is* a person, and this is a most perfect example of transference of human characteristics to an inanimate object. Whether or not a boat is an inanimate object is, of course, open to question; my objection to depicting boats as people cannot be sustained with any great conviction when I consider our almost maudlin affection for our own boats. It is probably the degree of affection that a writer has for his subject that determines how successfully he can convey the flavor of a personality, and there is no doubt that Hardie Gramatky loves Little Toot, the bad boy of the river, who gloriously becomes the hero. There is such gusto in the pictures, and such forthrightness in the manner of telling the story that the reader, especially if he is a little boy, is captivated at once. It is all ridiculously funny, especially to a grown-up, but there is scarcely time to laugh because events move at a breathless pace, and before you have quite finished reading the last page the little listener flips the book over and says, "Now, read it again." The other day our young man shared somebody's birthday, and was given a nice square sturdy little tug-boat, just enough like Little Toot to pass muster. That night when we went to tuck him in, we found him sleeping with his boat clutched fast in his arms, and as we gently moved it away, he stirred in his sleep and murmured, "Where's Little Toot?" We felt that Hardie Gramatky was the real giver of the gift.

Curiously enough, we have had almost no fun at all with books about automobiles or airplanes. For one thing, there are scarcely any good ones, and for another the actual experience of just seeing them seems to satisfy our little mechanic. He marches into the public library imperiously demanding "a book about cars or an airplane book," and usually comes away with something that he thinks he wants, but nothing so far has held his interest for very long except Lois Lenski's *The Little Auto* and *The Little Aeroplane,* which he deeply loves although they haven't anything like the character of *The Little Train.*

Two picture-books that have a variety of things that go caught our young friend's imagination when he was still small enough to want very little in the way of text or story for his pictures, and they are still lots of fun. Clement Hurd's *The Race* is a clever bit of story-telling in pictures, with just enough words to satisfy a small companion that he is really being read to. A duck and a monkey engage in contest to see who can get home first, and you follow through a series of drawings in clear, bold outline and rich flat color, the breathless tale of their resourceful use of every form of transportation that happens along. Happy reunion with family and friends is the satisfactory climax of the tale.

H. A. Rey's *How Do You Get There?* has no story, but is a sort of trick book: a third of each page is folded in, and when you first look at it, you see a picture of people about to go on a journey, or someone waiting for someone else to arrive. Each picture has a legend describing the situation, and ending with, "How will they get there?" Then you open the page out full, and the hitherto concealed part of the drawing is the answer. The device is simple enough for little hands to cope with, and the pictures are so full of zest, color and humor that they are still, after these many months, good for happy crows of surprise and pleasure.

Soon after we had got started at the job of satisfying our young man's appetite for books about locomotion, we realized that there were several points that we must be careful about. One was that we should not allow books to take the place of experience with mechanical things, and thus act as a limiting agent; another, that wherever mechanical terms were used, or where the pictures were intended to instruct, both must be accurate. The third and very important one was that there should be enough really good books, well written, with humor and provocativeness, to stimulate him and to lead him into enjoyment of literature concerned with a wider range of subjects. Apparently he had the same idea, for with the exception of the matter of accuracy, he has taken our program into his own hands. It has been a fine education particularly for me, to be responsible for verifying the authenticity of an author's exposition or an artist's pictures of a train or a boat or any of the other means of locomotion. It may seem a bit far-fetched, to be concerned about the reliability of the information that a very small boy gathers up from story- and picture-books. But it seemed to us that when his interests were so positively mechanical he ought to be protected from the wastefulness of inaccurate information or impression, and we needed to train ourselves to be critical. So far no very knotty problems have come up, but we are learning to find out *how* to find out, and when his reading takes him beyond the limits of our own scientific knowledge, we hope to be able to direct him to the proper means of determining the authenticity of what he reads. It is surprising how often we find among our acquaintances people who are authorities on some specialized branch of knowledge, and they, being enthusiasts, like to be consulted. Then there are good standard sources of information at the public library; and if we ever find ourselves quite at sea to know what is correct and what is not, it seems to me that it will be quite permissible to discover and consult a good authority on the matter in hand. If a little boy's rapturous enthusiasm for cars and trains and boats should by any chance develop into a maturer concern with any form of mechanical knowledge, we want that knowledge to be sound and his vocabulary adequate and exact.

If we ever had any idea that our baby might show a tendency to let books satisfy his curiosity about land, water and air transport, it evaporated rapidly under the warmth of his eagerness to see and examine at first hand. Cars, trucks, snow-plows, tractors, fire-engines, airplanes, all are a source of endless excitement to him. We make a point of giving him every possible chance to make closer acquaintance with them.

As for trains: Saturday afternoon is our time for going in a body to the public library, and it has been a wonderful arrangement for our littlest member. If we time our movements well, we can have an hour or so among the books, helping each other to choose what we shall take home, and taking a good look round to be sure we are not missing anything. Then we walk across the road and stand on the railroad bridge. First of all we see two local trains, one northbound and one going into the city. They stop at the station to let off and take on passengers, while we survey from above all the pleasant activity of greetings and farewells, the handling of heavy boxes and baggage, and the exasperated efforts of the conductors to get everybody on board. Just as the clouds of smoke have cleared away after the southbound train goes under the bridge, a trolley car comes ambling up the outside track with a rather discouraged air. We can hear it bump to a stop just out of sight, and then after a short interval it gathers itself together with a rattle and trundles out of hearing. Sometimes a hand-car comes along, and the men wave to us as it scoots under the bridge. And then comes the real event of the day: The "Four Hundred," often with as many as fifteen brilliant yellow, green-roofed cars, comes streaming out of the south and charges along beneath us with a magnificent roar. We watch it out of sight, flashing along under the bridges and vanishing into the distance with breathtaking speed. "Well!" we say, "Wasn't that fun?" And our wee boy clutches his train books under his arm, and trots contentedly along to help with the week-end shopping.

Sometimes we vary the routine, and go down the steps to the station platform to see the trains come in and out; or we may go to watch a freight-train being shunted onto the coal company's siding. There is always something new and exciting for our little companion to see, and he misses nothing because his books have helped him to know what to look for.

He knows the inside of trains, too. Two long trips last summer gave him the chance to explore and examine to his heart's content. Just a fortnight ago he had the greatest adventure of all, a day's excursion to Milwaukee on the "Four Hundred." And the next day, when he was reading *The Little Train,* it was not the Blue Streak Express that went whizzing by, but "a big yellow 'Four Hundred,' taking me to Milwaukee."

He knows from his own experience too, that "there is nothing—absolutely nothing half so worth doing as simply messing about in boats." For three blissful summer months he is in and out of boats all day long, looking and listening and doing and learning and having a gloriously good time. Here, too, what he has heard from books and seen in their pictures gives a special perceptiveness to his view of life on the water, and his own experience invests his books with reality and importance. Each without the other would be fun, but together they create a resource and imaginative energy that sustain and perpetuate delight.

It has been interesting to watch the development of book sense in our small son. Perhaps the fact that his estimate of a book has so often coincided with our own has led us to give him credit for greater judgment than he actually possesses. It may be, too, that our reluctance to read very frequently books that we find dull, has had something to do with his indifference to them. But I think we have been reasonably open-minded, and have given him a chance to sample a great variety of books, and to show his own pleasure or lack of interest. So it is not extravagant to say that he has a certain discrimination in choosing books for his own enjoyment. He likes directness of narration, and is impatient with "too much words." He has an instinctive mistrust of sentimentality. He enjoys good honest humor, but does not like forced funniness. And he makes no response whatever to stories that are artificial. All of this is just what we hoped for, and while it might very well be that we had unconsciously influenced his taste just by not providing definitely poor books for his own library, I think it is quite true that even with books limited in subject as these have been, he has found a pretty well-balanced diet of the fact and fantasy and fun that are a part of good literature.

I confess that we began to have some doubts of his ever branching off into books about anything other than trains and boats and cars, when he had got well into his fourth year without showing any sign of expanding his interests. Even now we are a bit crestfallen when he makes his usual request at the library for some book that he has already had a dozen times. But you have only to listen to his conversation to know that he begins to have a wide acquaintance with all sorts of books.

The broadening view began to appear last summer. We had taken several of Beatrix Potter's books to the cottage with us, just on the chance that he might begin to reach out for new ideas, and one afternoon, when he came scrambling up the path from the water, "shedding buttons right and left," I had a sudden vision of Tom Kitten coming up the rockery in like manner. He was ready for a "little relax," so I took him on my lap and showed him the pictures in *The Tale of Tom Kitten,* very casually at first, and ready to shift to another form of amusement if he showed the slightest impatience. But I need not have been so diffident; he settled down at once, listened to the whole story and looked at the pictures with the greatest interest. A day or two later we read *The Tale of Peter Rabbit* and that was even better. He asked for it every day and began to use words and phrases that pleased him. Picture our delight when we found him one morning, crouched down on the rocks by the water, peering anxiously at one of his little boats that had got washed in under a log, and saying, "I implore you to exert yourself!"

He has a great liking for the sound and feel of words, partly natural, and partly developed through listening to rhymes and poetry from his earliest babyhood. This, I think, is one reason why he so especially likes Beatrix Potter's books; she uses words so beautifully. He knows half a dozen of her books now, and his conversation is full of piquant phrases: "That dog won't play with me. I am affronted"; "I ran very fast, and my heart went lippity lippity not very fast"; "Theres' a fly on the window! Shuh, shuh, little dirty feet!" When he spilled a load of pebbles that he was hauling in his little train, he exclaimed in vexation, "What is the explanation of these showers of nuts!"

Our daughter has enjoyed almost more than any of us this broadening of his interest in books, for now she is able to share her library with him. *Little Black Sambo* and *Sambo and the Twins* have changed ownership—"After all, they're much more suitable for a little boy, Mummy"—and he is a constant and responsible borrower, returning books carefully to her shelves when he has finished reading them. He has not by any means lost his interest in mechanical books, but his growing up seems to have expanded his capacity to include our interests to a much greater extent than before, and this brings an added pleasure to our family relationships.

We have been amused to find that with two of his new books, which a year ago would have been valued exclusively for their pictures of things on wheels, his interest is turning more and more to descriptions and pictures of natural things. Lois Lenski's *The Little Farm* made its first appeal because of the drawings of farm machinery, and the first time we went driving in the country after he had got the book, he saw Farmer Small's tractor and Farmer Small's bobsled everywhere. But last week he saw Farmer Small's cornfield and his chickens and cows, and never a tractor at all, though it was much more in evidence than during the winter. At first, when he played at being Farmer Small, he ran the tractor and drove the car; but now he "catches apples" and "picks eggs" and sells vegetables at his roadside stand.

Virginia Lee Burton's *The Little House* has all sorts of mechanical things in it, automobiles and steam-shovels and trucks and an elevated train; and these were and still are, of great interest. But the loveliness of the countryside and the beauty of the changing seasons shine so radiantly from the pages that even a masculine four-year-old falls under the spell. There is something very touching in hearing a little boy reading to himself about the little house that was "curious about the city" until it grew up all around her, destroying her field full of daisies and shutting the moon and stars away from her. There is distress in his voice as he tells about the noise and dust and smoke, and the people hurrying past without even a glance at the poor shabby little house; and warm satisfaction when she is taken back again to the country and set upon a hilltop, to be lived in and loved once more. *The Little House* is a beautiful book, with a soundness of philosophy in both story and pictures that I think will leave a deep impression on the mind of the happy child who lives with it.

His experience of growing affection for and appreciation of *The Little House* is the history in miniature of his life with books. Fascinated interest in mechanical things led him into it, and opened up the way to the serviceable pleasure and perennial delight of "apple trees dancing in the moonlight."

CHAPTER FIVE

Poetry in the Nursery

OUR daughter is nine years old, an independent age. If she felt inclined, she could reject the whole idea of poetry. But when you ask her to choose a bedtime book "to be read to out of," as likely as not she will ask for William Blake. "Piping Down the Valleys Wild" and "Jerusalem" are her two favorites, and you have only to watch her face to know that she *really loves* those poems. This is not because she is different from the average run of children, nor because she is peculiarly a "poetic child." (It is simply because she lives with two people who take poetry, along with books and music and all beautiful things, as major blessings; and who believe in sharing these things with children as freely and casually as daily bread. The boy in the family is a rollicking lad, a man of action. He is being exposed to the same kind of thing in the same kind of way, and his response is different from that of his sister at an equal age only in manner: her delight was rapt and quiet, his is a froth of ebullience.

It is never too soon to begin to speak poetry to a baby. Probably you will do it at first for your own pleasure, just as you sing to him for the delight of watching his response. And it is not surprising to find yourself speaking poetry that is not included in any collection of Verses for the Littlest Ones. What could be more absurd than to say, as you tilt up a little chin to scrub under it, "Lift up your heads, O ye gates, and be ye lifted up, ye everlasting doors, that the King of Glory may come in"? But there is no buffoonery about it, and when a two-year-old gives you back those words with grave and touching pleasure, you feel that somehow he begins to know not only nobility of language, but something of the mystery and magnificence that lies behind it.

I cannot remember when Mother Goose first came into our nursery, but certainly when she arrived she found herself in good company. Shakespeare was there, to see a sleepy baby tucked in with:

> We are such stuff as dreams are made on,
> And our little life is rounded with a sleep.

If it was in the afternoon, "our little life" was "rounded with a nap," and the poetry lost nothing of its dignity from being translated into a tiny girl's vocabulary. St. Francis was there, presiding over the bath:

> Praised be my Lord for our sister Water,
> Who is very serviceable unto us,
> And humble and precious and clean.

William Blake was there, and A. E. Housman, and many another poet no less loved by a small person who, while she did not understand the words, still felt their sweetness and enjoyed their sound.

No nursery is complete without a good Mother Goose, a generous collection for mother and father, with "all the old songs that ever I heard of, and some that I don't know, like Whittington's Bells." Long before the baby's hands are strong enough to hold a volume of any size, or his eyes ready to focus on pictures, the routine of bathing and dressing and eating is enlivened by rhymes, chanted, said or sung. Was there ever a baby who would not chuckle over, "This little pig went to market" or "Dance, Thumbikin, dance"; who would not find the putting on of shoes less tedious with, "Shoe the old horse, shoe the old mare"; would not forget that he was tired of poached egg, when each spoonful approached ceremoniously with,

> Knock at the door,
> Peep in,
> Lift the latch
> and WALK IN!

The practice of avoiding friction wherever possible in training up the young in the way they should go has saved much wear and tear on the nerves of both mother and child. Here Mother Goose is an ever-present help. Not only is the attention of a rebellious little individual diverted from destructive activity; frustrated energy is turned eagerly and positively to the enjoyment of droll situations and dramatic happenings, and incidentally to the learning of new words and lively expressions. The theory of original sin in many a temperish situation evaporates almost comically under the

administration of treatment no more drastic than a dramat-
ically whispered,

> Little Boy Blue, come, blow your horn!
> The sheep's in the meadow, the cow's in the corn!

Then, in quiet surprise,

> Where's the boy that tends the sheep?

And as often as not a little voice will supply the answer,

> He's under a haycock, fa-a-a-st asleep.

There is a wonderfully persuasive quality in the nonsense
of the nursery rhymes. The tears that follow a tumble from
the high-chair soon give way to rainbow smiles with,

> Humpty Dumpty sat on a wall,
> Humpty Dumpty had a great fall,
> All the King's horses and all the King's men
> Couldn't put Humpty Dumpty together again.

—lately emended in our family to "Dumpty Dumpty had a
great crying—all better now." And when an insouciant
young gentleman steps off into thin air and rolls down the
staircase, "Jack and Jill," plus a very small bit of brown
paper soaked in imaginary vinegar, soon repairs the damage.
Every day while the potato is baking for lunch, we go
walking; and my small companion has established the custom of filling overall pockets with acorns, pebbles and other
small objects suitable for dropping through the grille over
a storm-sewer that we pass on the way home. No promise of

good lunch to come was sufficient to lure him away from the enchantment of hearing acorns plop into the dark water far below. Then one day inspiration suggested

> To market, to market
> To buy a fat pig

with galloping steps inviting in the direction of home. It worked like a charm, and now we have a whole repertoire of verses guaranteed to bring us tittuping along before the potato burns: "This is the way the ladies ride," "Ride a cock horse," "Four-and-twenty tailors," "Ride away, ride away, Johnnie shall ride," "Leg over leg as the dog went to Dover," "Here goes my lord, a-trot, a-trot, a-trot," and even "Dance to your daddie," with the last line changed for our purpose to, "You shall get a fishy when *we* come home."

There is in all this no solemn searching for suitable verses for all occasions—they are suddenly just there. When people tell me that their children do not care for this kind of thing, I remember that Lawrence Alma-Tadema suggested the source of the trouble when he said: "Do you know what is wrong with people who never read nursery rhymes? I will tell you. When little boys and girls grow bigger and older, they should always grow from the outside, leaving a little baby in the middle; even when they are quite grown up, the little child that once they were should be within them. But some unlucky people grow older from the inside, and so grow old through and through."

Nursery rhymes are alive and sparkling, not by grace of the printed page, but because they come by human speech, passed along from one generation to another, a sort of daisy chain linking the human family in loving enjoyment of living and playing together.

Then there are all the verses by the spiritual successors of Mother Goose, people like Robert Louis Stevenson, A. A. Milne, Eleanor Farjeon, Walter de la Mare, Christina Rossetti, Eugene Field, Elizabeth Coatsworth—a whole host of them who feel with sensitiveness and affection all the lovely surprise that a child finds in common, ordinary, everyday things. Not all of their verses are real poetry; but many a slight verse takes on genuine importance because of the way it lights up a little occasion, or provokes laughter, or just because of the pleasant sound of it. I do not think that Sturge Moore's "Beautiful Meals," for instance, is a fine poem. But when our first listener was three we used to say it:

> How nice it is to eat!
> All creatures love it so
> That they who first did spread,
> Ere breaking bread,
> A cloth like level snow,
> Were right, I know. . . .

How pleasantly Mr. Moore traces the development of the Art of Laying the Table; how delicately and engagingly he suggests the social responsibilities of breaking bread together! The saying of those lines invested our simple mealtime ritual with a new grace, gave it background, so to speak. And—what is the particular and pungent pleasure of sharing poetry—it added certain phrases to our family idiom, and gave us that warmly intimate "we have a secret, just we three" feeling that comes when a handful of people talk the same language.

There is the greatest fun in pointing up familiar things and everyday occasions with verses of this kind, which, because of the pattern of words and the singing of rhymes, are easily and happily tucked away in the memory. The other day our daughter found a tiny shell which, she was told, had come from the sands at Longniddry, a half hour's drive from Edinburgh. She pondered for a moment and then remembered:

> When I was down beside the sea
> A wooden spade they gave to me
> To dig the sandy shore.
> My holes were empty like a cup,
> In every hole the sea came up
> Till it could come no more.[1]

A five-year-old memory of "sun and wind and beat of sea" grew into completeness; she spoke of the red paint that came off the spade handle onto her hands, of the slippery feel of the sea-weed, of the "wild smell" of the sea, and the twinkle of the sun on the ripples as the tide came in.

Little children have such a wonderful generosity in accepting. I don't suppose, for instance, that there was much intrinsic fun in hearing Christina Rossetti's "Who has seen the wind?," that day when I first said it to a small boy with blown hair. But he enjoyed it because I did. And how we

---

[1] Robert Louis Stevenson· "At the Seaside."

both enjoyed it when he came galloping in from his play one boisterous morning, shouting, "The wind is passing froo, Mum, the wind is passing froo!" We see a robin, and out pops:

> Rollicking robin is here again!
> What does he care for the April rain?
> Care for it? Glad of it! Doesn't he know
> That the April rain carries off the snow,
> And coaxes out leaves to shelter his nest,
> And washes his pretty red Easter vest,
> And makes the juice of the cherry sweet
> For his hungry little robins to eat?
> > "Ha! ha! ha!" hear the jolly bird laugh,
> > "That isn't the best of the story by half!" [1]

A day or two later we hear, "Doesn't he know?" and, "Hear the jolly bird laugh!" quoted quite incongruously, but with relish. Tea-time, and the family cozily gathered around the fire, prompts some one to say:

> When the tea is brought at five o'clock,
> And all the neat curtains are drawn with care,
> The little black cat with bright green eyes
> Is suddenly purring there.[2]

And soon a picture of a pussy is greeted with, "Suddling purring there!"

One of the nice things about little children is their candid egocentricity. They like verses about how the world works to provide for their needs:

[1] Lucy Larcom: "Sir Robin."
[2] Harold Monro. "Milk for the Cat."

The friendly cow all red and white
I love with all my heart.
She gives me cream *with all her might*
To eat with apple-tart! [1]

and

Far down in the meadow the wheat grows green,
And the reapers are whetting their sickles so keen,
And this is the song that I hear them sing
While cheery and loud their voices ring:
" 'Tis the finest wheat that ever did grow,
And it is for Alice's supper, ho! ho!" [2]

Clothes are important, too. Anyone who remembers taking
his new shoes to bed with him understands a child's enjoyment of

William has some new pajamas,
Yellow cotton striped with brown,
And he says that when he wears them
He's a tiger lying down.

We are wakened in the morning
By a fearful, hungry roar,
And the brown and yellow tiger
Plunges through our bedroom door.

He says he's going to eat us—
We are terrified! But then
The tiger peels his skin off—
He's our little boy again. [3]

[1] Robert Louis Stevenson: "The Cow."
[2] Laura E. Richards· "Alice's Supper."
[3] A home-made jingle—fun for the family.

or

My paws are like a kitten's
When I wear my Sunday mittens
Which are lovely, fluffy white
Angora wool.

I can stretch them nice and wide,
So my thumb can come inside
To cuddle with my fingers,
When I pull.[1]

So much of the trivia that grown-ups take for granted is new and interesting to little children, and the range of verses in praise of it is almost endless. Much of the best of it has been written too recently for mothers and fathers to remember it from their own little days, so this is a field that requires some research. A good anthology of verses for children belongs in every family library, and it makes excellent "escape" reading. Propped up over the ironing-board, or open beside you as you do the household mending, it yields a fine harvest, easily committed to memory, of all sorts of jolly verses—the kind that help with the endless training in habits of cleanliness and good manners, story poems, nonsense rhymes, verses about pets and toys and the life out-of-doors, and quiet bedtime verses. Not all of them will appeal to the children as much as they do to you, but it is fun to have a mental scrapbag of one's own. It is better to say from memory rather than to read verses. I remember the first time I read a poem to my own four-year-old daughter—she covered the page with her

[1] A home-made jingle.

hands and said, *"Say* it, Mummy, *say* it!" I realized then that she had probably thought I had the gift of rhymed conversation, and was suitably flattered.

It is not long before a child's world takes on a new dimension. He has imaginary playmates—our current pair are named Liver and Ohio!—who are faithful good company. And he performs certain little rituals, like stopping to tap and listen at a particular tree that he passes on his walks, or sitting in unaccustomed silence on a special stair step, "being," as he says, "the music in the radio." This is the beginning of creative imagining. It is not that the magic has worn off his common world, but that he is becoming aware, without really knowing it, of things beyond his seeing. Now he listens with delight to:

> Some one came a-knocking
> At my wee small door,
> Some one came a-knocking,
> I'm sure—sure—sure;
> I listened, I opened,
> I looked to left and right,
> But nought there was a-stirring
> In the still, dark night. . . .[1]

He begins to be interested in things less tangible but no less real than have concerned him heretofore. Instead of thinking of a star as just a "little light away up there," he wonders what it is, and why. He wonders where he came from, what makes the wind blow, who made cows—all the speculations that are the concern of real poetry.

[1] Walter de la Mare: "Some One."

Some of the poetry that touches upon these things in a manner congenial to a little child he will have in the traditional bedtime prayers and "grace before meat," the really lovely ones, like:

> Here a little child I stand,
> Heaving up my either hand,
> Cold as paddocks though they be,
> Lord, I lift them up to Thee:
> For a blessing now to fall
> On our meat, and on us all.[1]

and

> Matthew, Mark, Luke and John,
> Bless the bed that I lie on.
> Four corners to my bed,
> Five angels there be spread,
> Two at my head,
> Two at my feet,
> And one at my heart,
> My soul to keep.

These, if they are to be more than a conventional gesture, should be shared between parent and child as a sort of common awareness of the power and the glory. They are, as some one said, "courtesies to the Almighty," the gentle acknowledgment of loving kindness.

One of the most comforting things I have heard lately was a teacher's reply when he was asked how children could be given security in upsetting times like these: "The only thing I can be sure of is that we must give them beauty in every

[1] Robert Herrick.

form we can discover. For my own part, I am teaching every class as if it were for the last time." It seems a far cry from Mother Goose and poems in praise of everyday things to civilian morale and the welfare of children in time of war. But if poetry is a part of one's own inner resources, what could be more natural than to share its "merry serviceableness"? Not every child will respond; some may not have the kind of perceptiveness that poetry requires. But I think it a pity to leave out of any child's experience *the chance to discover* what delight and comfort it can be.

CHAPTER SIX

Poetry for Children

"Not the Rose, but the Scent of the Rose"

BY the time our daughter was five years old, we had begun to interlard the "everyday" verses with more spacious poetry. Now I am just as much at a loss to define what I mean by this as A. E. Housman was when he was asked to define poetry in general: "I can no more define poetry than a terrier can define a rat. We both recognize the object by the symptoms which it provokes in us." What our family calls "grand poetry" is recognizable by the symptoms he describes, "a shiver down the spine," "a precipitation of water to the eyes," and "borrowing a phrase from Keats' Letters, where he says, speaking of Fanny Brawne, 'everything that reminds me of her goes through me like a knife.'" It is doubtful whether any child feels these symptoms acutely; doubtful, too, if it is desirable that he should. But if they are present in the parent's response, and if, as a result of them, an almost involuntary gift is made to the child, there is bound to be some communication of the thrilling pleasure. How otherwise can you account for the fact that after once hearing it said, a very little girl will beg, "Say that again about 'On a

cloud I saw a child,' " and listen as many times as you care to
say it, with grave and pleased attention?

William Blake has been for us a household delight. "Little
Lamb, Who Made Thee?" "Tiger, Tiger, Burning Bright,"
"When the green woods laugh with the voice of joy"—thèse
are full of innocent truth and shining beauty for the child,
and full of refreshment for the "tired heart." Our child's use
of them has not been without drollery: the question once
came up in the family of differences between white and
colored folk, and we read together "The Little Black Boy."
Some time later a zealous lady came to call, soliciting support
for an organization designed to protect the interests of "100
per cent Americans" against the encroachments of "foreign-
ers." Mamma, somewhat nettled by the assumption that she
might ever identify herself with so unimaginative a project,
replied flatly and somewhat unkindly that she herself was
not American-born. Whereupon the caller, to cover her confusion, turned to the small girl present at the interview, and
inquired brightly, "And where were you born, Dolly?"—
only to be plunged into still deeper discomfort by the star-
tling reply,

> My mother bore me in the southern wild,
> And I am black, but O! my soul is white!

The use of poetry in this family is frequently, I am sure,
what some might call indiscriminate. But I do not think it
would trouble A. E. Housman, for instance, to see a small
girl, ruffled and cross because of having to get up before she
was ready, beguiled into tranquillity with:

Yonder see the morning blink,
The sun is up, and up must I
To wash and dress and eat and drink,
And look at things, and talk and think
And work, and God knows why.

Oh often have I washed and dressed,
And what's to show for all my pain?
Let me lie abed and rest:
Ten thousand times I've done my best,
And all's to do again.[1]

It is simply a way of saying, "Now look here, we're all in this business together—let's make the best of it"; not, I think, a dangerous doctrine of futility. The rebellion at early bedtime is smoothed over with Edna St. Vincent Millay's:

Was it for this I uttered prayers,
And sobbed and cursed
And kicked the stairs,
That now, domestic as a plate,
I should retire at half-past eight! [2]

To be sure, Eleanor Farjeon has taken care of the whole situation with:

It's a singular thing that Ned
Can't be got out of bed.
When the sun comes round

[1] A. E. Housman: Number IX in *Last Poems.*
[2] Edna St. Vincent Millay: "Grown-up."

He is sleeping sound,
With the blankets over his head.

.   .   .   .

It's a singular thing that Ned,
After the sun is dead
And the moon's come round,
Is not to be found,
And can't be got into bed.[1]

But somehow the others seem to fit the circumstances more
pertinently, so why not use them?

Just as the words came up to me
I sang them . . .

and it is this very spontaneity that has given zest and variety
to our use of poetry as common coin. It is an extraordinary
thing how trivial an incident invites a poetic decoration: a
little girl, watching her mother fasten on a necklace, asks,
"What are those beads made of, Mum?"; and you reply:

Nymph, nymph, what are your beads?
Green glass, goblin. Why do you stare at them?
Give them me.
No.
Give them me. Give them me.
No.
I will howl all night in the reeds,
Lie in the mud and howl for them.
Goblin, why do you love them so?
They are better than stars or water,

[1] Eleanor Farjeon: "Ned."

Better than voices of winds that sing,
Better than any man's fair daughter,
Your green glass beads on a silver ring.
Hush, I stole them out of the moon.
Give me your beads, I desire them.

　　　　　　　　　　　　No.

I will howl in a deep lagoon
For your green glass beads, I love them so.
Give them me. Give them.

　　　　　　　　　　　　No.[1]

Once, on the day of the first snow, we read together the One Hundred and Forty-seventh Psalm, because of the memorable verse, "He giveth snow like wool, and scattereth the hoarfrost like ashes." Out of that came one of the warmest tributes I have ever had: the children in our daughter's grade at school were discussing which of two Psalms they should choose to memorize for a Thanksgiving exercise, and our representative cast her vote for "O give thanks unto the Lord," "because," she explained, "I already know 147." "I'll bet you don't," came the challenge. And away went the challenged:

Praise ye the Lord, for it is good to sing praises unto our God.
For it is pleasant, and praise is comely.
The Lord doth build up Jerusalem, he gathereth together . . .

　"All right, all right, you know it! How?"
　"My mother read it to me that day it snowed."
　"You mean your mother *reads you the Bible?*"

[1] Harold Monro: "Overheard on a Saltmarsh."

"Of course," this without a trace of swagger or self-consciousness. "My mother reads me all the good books."

How pleasant to have an eight-year-old accept the Bible, so rich a source of magnificent poetry, as a *good book!*

A spring day, and fruit blossoms against the sky, evokes "Loveliest of trees, the cherry now"; there is magic, on a frosty, starry night, in Robert Graves' "Are you awake, Gemelli?"; the sight of a little old lady, walking in the dusty grass by the roadside, stirs up the remembrance of Padraic Colum's "An Old Woman of the Roads," with its warm compassion for "poor mortal longingness." And how often and often have we said:

> Look thy last on all things lovely
> Every hour. Let no night
> Seal thy sense in deathly slumber
> Till to delight
> Thou have paid thy utmost blessing.
> Since that all things thou wouldst praise,
> Beauty took from those who loved them
> In other days.[1]

Meaning, *per se,* is a rather secondary consideration in our choice of poetry for sharing, for it is one of the subtlest and most valuable properties of great poetry that it speaks to the feelings rather than to the intellect. What for the moment has no applicable meaning for the child, because of his limited experience, is often committed readily and joyously to memory for the music of the words and the haunt-

---

[1] Walter de la Mare. "Farewell."

ing quality of the images. Years later, it will flower in all the nobility of its intention, to illuminate and enrich experience. James Stephens' "The Poppy Field," for instance, suggests a more penetrating sense of relative values than will concern the small listener, but a seed is dropped, along with the flowers. This is one of the concrete reasons why we feel that poetry is an essential to the full development of the child's spiritual faculties: memory is in the early years both receptive and tenacious, and if it is stored with "images of magnificence" there will be the less room for what is cheap and ugly. Then, too, familiarity with the language of genuine poetry gives breadth and color to the child's speech, and this in itself stimulates a sharpened perception of external beauties and spiritual truths.

We had never read any quantity of poetry together at one time until this past summer, rather choosing to point up a moment with an apt quotation, often just tossed into the air. But—how it came about I do not know—we found ourselves one evening exchanging verses with each other as we sat in the veranda watching the sun "sinking in the west," over the quiet water of Georgian Bay. It was exhilarating to find how one poem suggested another, and how our daughter lit up with pleasure at hearing lines already half familiar. We ran to fetch some books—John Drinkwater's *The Way of Poetry* and Edward Thomas' *Poems and Songs for the Open Air* were what we had on hand—and Herrick, Blake, Shakespeare, Stephens, Marlowe, Harold Monro and "Anonymous" were among those present at the inauguration of what Miss Duff, with a dramatic flourish, called our "Poetry

Evenings." Many a bedtime hour slipped by unheeded as we
bubbled lyrics old and new, sonnets, odes, soliloquies, bal-
lads and story-poems and Psalms. I think that when all the
other happenings of the summer have blurred into the
golden haze that surrounds all our holidays together, this
reading of poetry will come back as one of the most satisfying
and heart-stirring and reassuring episodes of all our happy
career. For the sharing of especially treasured poetry revealed depths and shades of character and attitude as few
things have ever done. To hear a nine-year-old girl-child
reading her two "most favorites," Blake's "Jerusalem," and
Harold Monro's "Real Property"; to see the expression on a
father's face as he gives her:

> I will make thee beds of roses
> And a thousand fragrant posies,
> A cap of flowers and a kirtle
> Embroidered all with leaves of myrtle,[1]

—these are "real property" of a richness vouchsafed to few
on earth!

"And oh, the merry laughter" that went with the reading
of "Widdicombe Fair"! We had never realized what superior nonsense it is, until we spoke it chorally, using every
vocal effect of which we were capable, and rising in a fine
crescendo to "OLD Uncle Tom Cobley and all!" at the end of
each verse. There really is some intoxication about nonsense
verse that is *real* nonsense. It defies all the laws of nature and
of art; it violates every canon, rule and statute of conven-

---

[1] Christopher Marlowe: "The Passionate Shepherd to His Love."

tional writing; it baffles invention and thumbs its nose at
analysis; it denies reality and laughs at common sense. And
there is healing in it, and sanity and health, for it reaches the
very source of innocent laughter. No childhood is complete
without it; children have an insatiable appetite for spontaneous fun, and families who have laughed till they cried over
"A Roundabout Turn," "The Poor Unfortunate Hotten-
tot," "The Owl and the Pussycat," "The Hunting of the
Snark," "The Old Sailor" and all the rest, have a solider
basis for intuitive understanding than psychological research
can discover. The fun of this kind of thing is peculiarly du-
rable, and is perennially renewed. Our nine-year-old came
home the other day with "The Walloping Window-blind," a
prime favorite with my own family when young. But it had
never seemed so richly funny as when she stood on one foot
and sang it, beginning with reasonable restraint that diminished rapidly with each absurdity, and dissolving into helpless laughter at "shot at the whistling bee."

We have never—or seldom—*read* nonsense verse in our
family. It is so subtle, and "comes in handy" at such unexpected moments that it should be on tap, without the limitations of print. One always feels that these verses were first
spoken or sung; their music is, as Laura Richards says, of the
hurdy-gurdy variety—whether you want it or not, it sticks
in the memory. And what fun, when a stray word or a provocative phrase brings the whole ridiculous, jingling, adorable song tumbling out to renew old laughter! Laura Richards, Lewis Carroll, Edward Lear, Robert Charles, Hilaire
Belloc, A. A. Milne—all the bright galaxy of nonsense-

makers—these are the darlings of the household that loves
its fun.

> What is poetry? Who knows?
> Not the rose, but the scent of the rose;
> Not the sky, but the light of the sky;
> Not the fly, but the gleam of the fly;
> Not the sea, but the sound of the sea;
> Not myself, but something that makes me
> See, hear, and feel something that prose
> Cannot; what is it? Who knows? [1]

And who is to say what line, what "gracious flight of words"
may fall, and take root, and grow and flower in the mind of
a child? Not to miss the chance of such burgeoning, we have
shared much of the poetry we know, and we have learned
much that we did not know before. Perhaps it will mean
nothing more than that we have shared delight, and in the
sharing have created something strong and good. But that is
enough.

Praise we therefore famous men . . . such as found out musical
tunes and recited verses in writing;
Rich men, furnished with ability, living peaceably in their habi-
tations;
All these were honored in their generations, and were the glory
of their times;
There be of them, that have left a name behind them, that their
praises might be reported. [2]

[1] Eleanor Farjeon: "Poetry."
[2] Ecclesiasticus XLIV.

CHAPTER SEVEN

Fun with Words

THE first time I ever heard a book recommended as "vo-cabulary-tested," I had just been reading A. P. Herbert's hilarious *What a Word!*, and I had a sudden vision of a book inoculated against infection by what he calls "septic verbs" and "toxic nouns." I asked what the term signified and was told that the vocabulary had been chosen to conform with a standard word list for pre-school children, approved by an educational committee with a very impressive sounding name.

Now I can quite understand the need for limiting the difficulty of words in a book used for teaching children to read, for reading is a skill that in the beginning requires the co-ordination of eye and brain in an unaccustomed way. But this was a book supposedly intended to entertain little people at an age when new words are as interesting as new toys; and as I read through it I could not find anything at all in the language either stimulating or diverting. It was as sober and uninteresting as rice pudding without any raisins. "The sort of book," I thought, "that no child of mine will ever have."

I believed then, and I believe even more firmly now, *that all words belong to children*. They choose them for their own use by the simple process of taking possession of the ones they need to express what they want to say. If children do not hear speech that has variety and liveliness, and if their books do not have unfamiliar words tucked in like bright little surprises among the everyday ones, how in the world are they ever to accumulate a store of language to draw on, as new experiences and sensations increase the need and desire to communicate with the people they live with? Children, like the rest of us, need to be articulate, and it seems to me a withholding of what is properly theirs, to limit their experience of words (as in the "vocabulary-tested" book) to the vocabulary already possessed by an "average" child of any given age.

Not that you can limit them really. Most children have a fine inventiveness, and make up words to fit objects whose proper names they do not know. But they are happier, I think, if they know the names that other people use; it must be a bit lonely, when you very eagerly want to share something, to find that the key word is in a language understood only by yourself. We have a good illustration of that in our family: when our wee boy was two-and-a-half, and we were spending our summer in Georgian Bay, every time our boat came out of a certain channel into a wide bay, he pointed away down the bay and talked in great excitement about the "ottatee." We tried and tried to discover what it was that he meant, but it is difficult to pick out one particular object in a wide expanse of island-set water, with only an uncertain small finger to point it out to you. We rather forgot about it during the following winter, but last summer, when he was three-and-a-half, the very first time we came to that particular stretch of water, he lunged to the side of the boat and exclaimed rapturously, "There's the dear ottatee again!" All summer he begged to go closer, and shed tears of real disappointment and frustration when we were totally unable to discover what it was that he wanted to see. He has begun to talk about it again, and one of our projects for his four-and-a-half-year-old summer will be to narrow the field of exploration until we find out just what the "ottatee" is and give him the common name for it. It may prove to be something like a Government Navigation Marker, a term which I am sure would not be included in any vocabulary-tested book for a four-and-a-half-year-old child, but if that is the proper term, he has a right to it. If he were still only two-and-a-half and we discovered that that was the label he needed for his beloved object, we would still give it to him. He might have a little trouble in saying it, but he would soon learn, and he would have the fun of being able to talk to us, so that we would understand, about something that really excites him.

Just as we always avoided "baby-talk," when our children were learning to talk, so we shunned the use of euphemisms and made-up expressions designed to sidestep our responsibility of teaching our children to hear and reproduce accurately the shape of human speech, and to use words precisely. Certainly they were not always able to manage the syllables clearly at first and we cherish the memory of their quaint and enchanting approximations. Little children have a spectacular ability to learn and we were bound to show our respect for their eagerness and competence by never fobbing off on them words that were an insult to their dignity as human beings. In our speech with them, and in the books we expose them to, we have tried to give them a pattern of good usage, because we believe that "words are living powers, . . . the vesture which thoughts weave for themselves," and that a careless and unimaginative use of words tends to destroy meaning. This, in turn, may lead to soft habits of thinking.

Our method—if you can call it that, when it is a simple, unself-conscious expression of ourselves—sounds as if it might be likely to turn children into "pretty prating parrots." On the contrary, it has given them and us more sheer fun than almost any other thing that I can think of. The most casual exchange of conversation has possibilities of surprise, and it is very pleasant to live with people whose common coin of expression seems always new-minted. Luckily for us, both of our babies took to words with all the delight of ducklings discovering the fun of swimming. They are both "collectors" of words, and their way of finding out the value of any "item" is to use it experimentally, sometimes with a very droll effect. Not long ago our ten-year-old came across "malevolent" in a context that did not make the meaning quite clear. So she tried it out on us. We were speculating at breakfast one morning about the possibility of living like the Swiss Family Robinson on our stern and rockbound Georgian Bay island, without any way of getting food except by our own efforts. Blueberries we would have, and fish, and mushrooms and edible fungi. They say porcupine meat is very good, and there must be quantities of edible roots, if you know where to look, and dandelion and dock leaves are excellent greens. But what should we do for bread? I elaborated a fanciful scheme for sowing a crop of wild oats, harvesting the grain, threshing it, and grinding it in the coffee mill. "Just think," said I, "of the delicious things we could make: oatcakes, and oatmeal cookies and bread, and the most ambrosial porridge!" "That," said our daughter enthusiastically, "sounds perfectly malevolent!" It seemed almost a pity to tell her what the word really means.

It is astonishing to find how quickly a child's working vocabulary grows and takes on color. Even when he appears to be paying no attention to a conversation, he gathers in words; and from hearing them in action, so to speak, he gets an idea of their meaning. Many of our favorite reminiscences about our children's early days are concerned with the unexpected expressions they have used. One tiny girl, aged two and a half, was given a suit of pajamas with pictures of nursery-rhyme people printed all over them. As she turned back the tissue paper wrapping she said, with unmistakable delight, "Are they beauteous! Are they charming!" We still remember the mingled surprise and pleasure on the faces of the two who had brought the gift. When our man-child was the same age he picked up an expression that gave him great social prestige: being a perfect whirlwind of activity, he found repose impossible, and one afternoon when we wanted to have tea in peace and quiet, I said in despair, "Oh, you have a superabundance of energy!" He seemed not even to hear me speak, but a day or two later he startled a group of his father's students by announcing that his name was "Superabundance of Energy." They still love to tell about it, and are impressed with the fact that he can use either of the big words quite correctly in other contexts.

But polysyllables are only the foam on the ale; the good sound brew of language is a mellow compound of words deftly chosen to convey the precise and subtle intention of the thought. You find it in good books for even very little children. Beatrix Potter's *Peter Rabbit* is an almost perfect example of fiction, according to G. K. Chesterton's uncompromising standard that "the psychology must be right, and every act must represent it rightly." And the writing is superbly clean and sure: Beatrix Potter uses one word where a less able writer would need three or four to convey the same sense, but there is an effect of effortless grace and flexibility in this subtle economy. Opening the book at random, you find "Peter gave himself up for lost, and shed big tears; but his sobs were overheard by some friendly sparrows, who flew to him in great excitement, and implored him to exert himself." There, in a nutshell, is a complete dramatic episode; the words were not taken from any approved list for pre-school children, but three-and-four-year-olds have an instinctive perception of the meaning. And how they love to use them!

In every one of Beatrix Potter's twenty-one works of fiction, from the minute-long tale of "The Fierce Bad Rabbit" to the hours of enchantment in *The Fairy Caravan*, there is

that same precise, economical, fertile use of words. A delicate understatement points up the reality of every character,
and the drollery of every situation. Every sentence has direction, clarity and flavor. Consider Mrs. Tittlemouse: she
"was a most terribly tidy particular little mouse, always
sweeping and dusting the soft sandy floors. Sometimes a
beetle lost its way in the passages. 'Shuh! Shuh! little dirty
feet!' said Mrs. Tittlemouse, clattering her dustpan." There
is a housekeeper for you!—she rises full-panoplied from one
short paragraph.

The same humorous penetration shows in: "Mrs. Tabitha
Twitchet dressed Moppet and Mittens in clean pinafores
and tuckers; and then she took all sorts of elegant, uncomfortable clothes out of a chest of drawers in order to dress
up her son Thomas." There is a wealth of suggestion in
those words "elegant, uncomfortable." And how sensitively
she underlines a contrast in characters. "Little Benjamin
said: 'It spoils people's clothes to squeeze under a gate; the
proper way to get in is to climb down a pear tree.' Peter fell
down head first; but it was of no consequence, as the bed below was newly raked, and quite soft." Little children find
this sort of thing very much to their taste; it fits into the
memory so neatly, and they have the fun not only of form-
ing delightful friendships with Beatrix Potter's beguiling
people, but of adopting into their own speech the words and
phrases that gives the stories such exuberance.

Her manner of using language that is pithy, imaginative,
and humorous creates zest and provocativeness and genuine
beauty in the more intricate adventures in *The Fairy Cara-*

van. Our daughter had loved the Peter Rabbit books from
the time she was two years old, and when her seventh birthday brought still another book by Beatrix Potter, more
grown-up, even, than *The Tale of Mr. Tod,* her cup of bliss
was full. I hope I shall never forget how she laughed herself
into hiccups when she read "the most gorgeous funny bit"
to us:

Pony Billy got out of the bog with a jump and a scramble up
the steep grassy slope of the hill. Round and round and round
he went underneath the oaks, always going widdershins, contrary to the sun; always leaving back-to-front misleading marks
behind him. Six times round he went; and he saw nothing but
the bluebells and the oaks. But the seventh time round he saw
a little Jenny Wren, chittering and fussing round an old hollow
tree. "What are you scolding, you little Jenny Wren?" She did
not stay to answer; she darted through the wood twittering
gaily. "I had better go and look inside that hollow tree myself,"
thought Pony Billy. He walked up to it and looked in. "Ho, ho!
What are you doing in there, Paddy Pig? Come out!" "Never
no more," replied Paddy Pig He was sitting huddled up inside
the tree, with his fore-trotters pressed against his tummy;
"never again. I cannot break through the ropes." "Ropes? don't
be silly! there is nothing but cobwebs." "What, what? no ropes?"
"Come out at once," said Pony William, stamping. "I am ill,"
replied Paddy Pig; he pressed his trotters on his waistcoat.
"What have you been eating?" "Tartlets." "Tartlets in Pringle
Wood! more likely to be toadstools. Come out, you pig; you are
keeping the circus waiting." "Never no more shall I return to
the go-cart and the caravan." Pony Billy thrust his head through
the spider-webs in the opening, seized Paddy Pig's coat-collar

with his teeth and jerked him out of the tree. "What, what? no ropes? but it is all in vain." He sat upon the ground and wept.

"Try a potato? I brought you some on purpose." "What, what? potatoes! but is it safe to eat them?" "Certainly it is," said Pony Billy. "They did not grow in Pringle Wood. Eat them while I have my nosebag. Then I will carry you home again pig-a-back." "We will be chased. And I will fall off." He ate all the potatoes; "I feel a little better; but I know I will fall off. Oh, oh, oh! Something is pinching my ears!"

Whatever might be the matter, Paddy Pig's behavior was odd. He got up on a tree-stump, and he tried to climb into the saddle. First he climbed too far and tumbled over the other side; then he climbed too short and tumbled; then he fell over the pony's head; then he fell backwards over the crupper, just as though something were pulling him. He sat upon the ground and sobbed, "Leave me to my fate. Go away and tell my friends that I am a prisoner for life in Pringle Wood." "Try once more. Sit straight, and hold on to the strap of lockets," said Pony Billy, trampling through the bluebells.

He came out from under the trees into the sunshine. He trotted across the green grass of the open meadow, and carried Paddy Pig safely back to camp.

If I should be limited to the books of one author for my children, I think I should certainly choose Beatrix Potter. I wish she could know how much exquisite pleasure she has given us, and how much of our children's delight in their mother-tongue they owe to her.

When our daughter was still little, we could be fairly sure that she knew the meaning of all the words she encountered, for she heard most of them from us and from the books we read to her. But she learned to read quickly, and so easily that there was some chance that she might fall into the lazy habit of sliding over unfamiliar words with only an approximate idea of what they meant. So she was not very old when we drew her into our practice of consulting the dictionary whenever any question came up of the meaning, use, or derivation of a word. It is truly amazing how often this happens when you take a great interest in the subtle shades of language. Until she became able to find her way around in the fine print of our big dictionary, we looked up words with her, showing her how to figure out the pronunciation from the accent marks and the key to vowel sounds at the foot of the page. This was good fun, and she was soon a real dictionary addict.

—We had found that discussions of words came up so frequently at mealtimes that one or other of us was always running for the dictionary, until finally it occurred to us that it would save considerable confusion if we simply considered it standard equipment for the dinner-table. This happened at the time when our child was beginning to have a share in the work of the household, and her responsibility was the table-setting. When she was still at the learning stage I would inspect the table to see that everything was in its proper place. Once I said, "You've forgotten the condiments" (that was a sort of "spoof" word with us, because of somebody's pun about "condimentia praecox"), and she asked, "What about the dictionary? Is that a condiment?" It did not occur to me at the time, but it really is, in its own definition of a condiment as "something to add relish to food."

For there was a great zest to our mealtime discussions, especially as our daughter's reading added more and more to her vocabulary. Our Sunday evening suppers were particularly gay; then we played word games, "I love my love with an A," and "What's another word for ——?" She loved to surprise us with new words, and would be in a fever of impatience for Sunday to come if she had found an especially good one. How we laughed, that time when we were playing "I love my love," and she counted around to see what her letter would be, almost exploding with mirth when she found that it was what she wanted. The moment came and she announced with gusto, "I love my love with an S because he's STYPTIC!"

She likes the shape and feel of words; I once remarked on the fragrance of a spray of sun-warmed juniper that she brought into the cottage, and she said, "Isn't fragrant a lovely word! I'd like to call my daughter Fragrant Anne." A day or two later she came across "torso" and liked the roundness of it; lapis lazuli was her favorite precious stone before ever she saw it, and all onomatopoeic words delight her, so that she makes nice use of them. She has quite a poetic turn of phrase too; the first time she saw a hummingbird, she captured the wonder of the moment in a beautifully simple description: "He hung above the flowers, moving in a mist of wings." She makes many little occasions memorable for us with just such sensitive words.

When she had reached the second grade, she began to talk about where words came from. The first word that ever

excited her interest was "anniversary." We told her about
the Latin words *annus*, a year, and *vertere*, to turn, and drew
a little picture showing the year marching up to a special
occasion like a birthday or a wedding anniversary, and then
turning to run down again on the other side. She considered
it gravely for a moment, and then said, "Latin is fun, isn't
it?" We reminded her of the wonderful afternoon we had
spent when she was five years old, watching the workers digging away at the remains of a Roman Villa that had been
discovered by archaeologists just inside the ancient city wall
of Dorchester in England. She had been a little mystified by
the idea of spending so much time and care "digging up an
old house." But she brought away a snail-shell, given her by
one of the workers who said it had been found in "the
Roman lady's rose-garden"; and an oyster-shell from the
kitchen rubbish-heap. These have increased in value as she
has learned something of British history, and when we told
her that Latin was the language spoken by the lady who
tended the garden and the man who ate the oyster, she was
interested at once. There is no resistance to classic languages
in that small brain. Her interest has served to sharpen ours,
and we have done much exploring together, the two "elders"
refreshing their memory of Latin literature, and drawing on
a fund of knowledge dust-covered and neglected for lo,
these many years.

The discovery that ancient ways of speech, now officially
consigned to the category of dead languages, are actually
very much alive in our words, has opened up a new and
fascinating field for our little philologist. We have talked

about how the English language has grown in scope and richness, like a river growing broader and deeper as tributary waters flow into it; and of how nothing is lost. The words that people used in times long gone to tell of important things have been gathered in and reshaped, like pebbles tossed about on the river's bed Not long ago she asked me, when she came in from school one day, if I realized that our word "meeting" came from the Anglo-Saxon word *mót*, the name of the council of the Ancient Britons. "Isn't it exciting that we've gone on being British for so long!" I like that feeling, that we are a part of all our heritage of race, and that the words we use are like little tough, persistent roots, securing us to the deep soil we spring from. It seems to me that it increases the sense of responsibility for the welfare of a world that has known human speech for such a long, long time, and I am glad that our daughter is growing toward the idea of herself as a steward of good human tradition.

We often find words that stem from the languages of other nations, and this leads us to consider how language reflects the history of the intermingling of peoples. After this war, we say, people will be bringing home words from all over the world, and they will grow into our speech so that we shall not even remember by and by that we have not always had them. "Do you suppose," asks our daughter, "that people will understand each other better, if they share each other's languages?" It is a satisfactory thing, to see how her robust enjoyment of the "apt and gracious words" of Kingsley and Kipling, Howard Pyle and Hans Andersen, Charles Lamb and Kate Seredy and Arthur Ransome, all the goodly company of her favorite story-tellers, is leading her to speculate on matters that are the concern of men of good will everywhere.

Our little man is still using words as playthings. Every day he finds new toys; today he came in to "collect" his mittens, and asked his father if "this coat is an advantage to you." He practices all by himself, getting the right sound, sense and function of each new word. I heard him as he trundled up and down the hall on his wooden horse: "Am I afraid of that boy? If he is bigger than me I am afraid of him, *otherwise* not." Now he demands, "Draw me a picture of that word," and studies the letters with a judicial air. Soon he will begin to read, and then comes the dictionary. After that who knows what new kinds of fun with words are in store for this family?

CHAPTER EIGHT

Lessons in Looking

Athree-year-old has a wonderful talent for just *looking!*
Watch him as he looks at a favorite picture-book,
turning a page rarely, and gazing with complete absorption
at pictures already familiar. His eyes travel appreciatively
from one detail to another, and when he moves on to the
next picture there is satisfaction in every line of his relaxed
little body.

I remarked quite lately on this leisured concentration to a
friend who dropped in one afternoon while our small boy
was engaged with *Johnny Crow's Garden,* curled up in a
little heap on the floor, and oblivious of all that was going
on around him. She apparently regarded my comment from
her point of view as a specialist in "junior psychology," and
quite took me by surprise by saying comfortingly, "I
shouldn't worry if I were you. We see many children not
much older than your boy who can study a picture for two
minutes and then name every object in it."

That was not what I meant at all; far from worrying, I
rejoice in the capacity for savoring the pleasure of pictures. I
agree that the ability to register what one sees is a useful and

necessary thing, but it is a one-dimensional faculty. The particular quality of a child's looking produces a far richer resource than cleverness at doing parlor tricks. He *takes possession* of pictures; they furnish his own private gallery with treasures that have no market value, but no collector can bid high enough to take them away from him.

That is the reason why it is so rewarding to choose really good and beautiful picture-books for a nursery connoisseur: he knows *how* to look at pictures. And if the "middle-man" knows how to provide him with material that combines appeal to his interest with genuine quality in line and color, he can begin early to establish a real standard. This innate ability to concentrate—I think you find it in almost all normal babies who are allowed quiet and solitude—seems to me a very positive and constructive advantage that should be preserved and strengthened by use. For it is another channel through which the spirit may be fed, another means of bringing the child into his own possession of the beauties that have been crystallized and made imperishable by the creative artistry of "men furnished with ability."

Our small daughter has always loved beautiful pictures, and has always had them to look at. Out of her enjoyment has come an enterprise of absorbing interest and delight for the whole family. One day we were reading *The Fairy Caravan*, and when we came to the lovely picture of sheep and lambs resting by the beck, it suddenly occurred to me that there was a very William Blake-ish quality in it. I got out some reproductions of the beautiful plates from *The Songs of Innocence* and we examined and compared the soft, ethereal colors, the brightness of the air, and the light, strong disposition of masses. We saw in the work of both artists qualities that we had never really *seen* before. My companion was genuinely interested, and I realized that her enjoyment and understanding of pictures had developed to a point where she might very profitably be introduced to some of the work of the master painters.

Very soon after that, Christmas began to gleam on the horizon, and Maud and Miska Petersham's *The Christ Child* came down from our daughter's bookcase to the living-room. We would look at those beautiful, glowing pictures almost every afternoon, and I hunted out the box in which we keep the loveliest Christmas cards of each year, hoping to find some reproductions of the Great Masters' paintings of Christmas subjects. There were three, Fra Angelico's *The Annunciation*, Botticelli's *The Nativity* and Paul Veronese's *Rest on the Flight into Egypt*. All of these were greeted with delight, both because the episodes they depict were familiar parts of a story that has gained in beauty and meaning with every telling, and because they are full of vitality, color and fascinating detail. She wanted more of the same kind of thing, and so it came about that whenever we happened on a reproduction of a good Christmas picture, in a magazine or on a postcard or a Christmas card, we would keep it against the next occasion when our small art-lover was in a suitable frame of mind to enjoy it. And that is how our family "art collection" was founded.

By the time that Christmas had rung its bells and gone, we had quite a respectable number of pictures put away in a big manila envelope. And we had developed, all three of us, a sharpened interest in pictures in general. Our daughter was still at the stage when she loved books with lots of pictures and, remembering how much she had enjoyed the experience of comparing Beatrix Potter's painting with William Blake's she would occasionally look for, or we might suggest, something to supplement what she found in her books. *Ferdinand* was our favorite funny book just then, and when I came across some of Goya's studies of bull-fights, I showed her the less grisly ones so that she could see how different they were from Mr. Lawson's pictures. She looked at them long and carefully, remarking on the fury and strength of the bulls, the tense swiftness of the man and the strange stormy light. "Golly, isn't it exciting?" she said, "I'd be afraid!" After that the pictures in *Ferdinand* seemed even funnier, because she was able to appreciate the full drollery of the burlesque—everything in *Ferdinand* seemed so merry and so *safe!*

The pictures in many other books, by their subject or style, suggested comparisons with the works of great painters. Hilda van Stockum's *A Day on Skates,* with its charming views of canals and houses and people, invited us to look at the paintings of The Dutch School: Pieter de Hooch's *The Linen Cupboard, The Interior of a Dutch House,* and *A Delft Courtyard;* Van der Burch's *The Terrace,* Vermeer's *The Cook,* Jan Steen's *A Domestic Scene* and Rembrandt's *Girl at the Open Half-door.* These pictures of the life of an earlier day in Holland have such a wealth of interesting detail in the clothes and the household

appurtenances, and such warmth and humor in the faces and
attitudes of the people that even a quite little girl was
charmed by them. Later on, when we had Hilda van Stockum's *Kersti and St. Nicholas,* we looked at Jan Steen's *The
Eve of St. Nicholas,* and *Twelfth Night Feast.* No jollier
scenes of family celebration could be found anywhere, and
our small girl, who has a great love of festival, was completely captured.

Just this last winter, when she was taken to see the Great
Dutch Masters Loan Exhibition, many of the canvasses were
familiar friends, and her excitement and delight at seeing
the originals were beautiful to see. She stood for a long time
before the *Twelfth Night Feast,* studying the happy faces in
the candlelight and reveling in the rich colors. "You know,
I've always loved that picture," she said. "But I didn't really
know how beautiful it was!" Then she moved along to the
Girl at the Open Half-door, and stood smiling up at the
bonny figure with the shy sweet face. "Oh, I just adore her!"
she exclaimed, "She's my very favorite!" I reminded her of
how we had first looked at the Dutch pictures because of
Hilda van Stockum's drawings, and she said, "Just think
what I'd have missed if I'd never had those books!"

Our collections of prints grew very rapidly during the
first few months, and at school our child was having a wonderful time with a teacher who had a splendid gift for stimulating and satisfying interest in pictures. One day our
daughter came home with news of the most beautiful book
of pictures, that her teacher had let her look at. She didn't
know its name, but her description of it was so glowing that

we asked her to find out. The next thing we knew, she was imploring us to give her for her eighth birthday her own copy of the wonderful book—Thomas Craven's *A Treasury of Art Masterpieces*. We considered it for a while, perfectly well aware that our inclination to grant the request came largely out of our pride in being the parents of a child who had such prodigious tastes for her age. Then we decided that even if it was an extravagance, and even if the desire was a more or less passing fancy, it would be a very good thing to have such a book for our own pleasure and edification as well as hers perhaps later on. So we bought it; and when she found it among the presents beside her place at breakfast on her birthday, she was speechless with delight. There was a new bicycle too, the gift of some friends whose daughter had outgrown it, and when she arrived from school that afternoon in the pouring rain I said, "I'm so sorry, you won't be able to ride your bicycle today." "Oh, I don't mind," was the reply, "I was going to look at my book anyway." And for two solid hours she sat and looked at her book. Scarcely a week has gone by since when she has not taken some time to look at her Art Masterpieces. She brings her friends home to look at it, marshaling them firmly to the bathroom first to wash their hands. And many and many a time I have looked into the living room, to see two small girls side by side on the couch, their feet sticking straight out in front of them, the book spread across the two laps, and two intent faces bent over the pictures. How glad we are now that parental pride won out over budgetary considerations.

The value of our daughter's picture-book training became more and more apparent as her knowledge of paintings grew. When she looked at Joshua Reynold's *The Age of Innocence,* she remarked that there was something in it that reminded her of Kate Greenaway's little girls—"She's so relaxed!" She commented on the difference between Beatrix Potter's rabbits and Dürer's; she felt that Dorothy Lathrop's drawings of *The Little Mermaid* had some of the same remote beauty as Botticelli's Venus—"I guess Botticelli does it better, but I do love *The Little Mermaid!*" She was seeing more and more what great artists were saying in their pictures, but her enjoyment of good illustrations in books was not one whit diminished. Occasionally she would come across a good book with pictures that did not satisfy her, and while she was quite capable of creating her own mental picture, and even making an attempt at getting it down on paper, it was great fun to keep an eye out for a good painting that caught her idea of what characters or scenes should look like. For instance, not long ago she came into possession of Margery Bianco's *Bright Morning,* which delighted her, but she said the pictures were "too thin." And one day when she was looking at a print of Renoir's *Little Girl with a Watering-Can,* she said, "That's Emmie—you know, in *Bright Morning.* She looks pretty quiet now, but you can tell that she's full of mischief."

Very often we would find pictures that seemed to her just right for the poems we read, and the songs we sang. I don't remember how we happened to read Wordsworth's "The Reaper," but I do know that I cannot think of it now without an image of Breton's *The Song of the Lark* coming to mind, for that was what our daughter immediately suggested as being the perfect picture of the poem. When we read Harold Monro's "Real Property," with the harvest-field described as "fifty acres of living bread," she said, "Isn't that like that picture of *The Gleaners?* I expect Millet was sitting in the shade of the hedge and the linden trees when he painted it."

She was always "tying up" pictures that she knew with music that she heard: "Now is the Month of Maying" was sometimes like Corot's *Dance of the Nymphs,* and sometimes like Breughel's *Rustic Wedding Dance. St. Nicholas a trois clériaux,* that wistful, haunting old song, always, for her, conjures up Gentile de Fabriano's *St. Nicholas Raising Three Youths from the Dead,* which we showed her the first time she heard the music; the simplicity and naïveté of the picture is so exactly what the song suggests. Time after time, she listens with particular pleasure to a song, or a piano piece or a symphony, and remarks how like it is to a certain painting. She can always explain the basis of these associations, and it gives us a very satisfying means of catching a glimpse of what goes on in her mind as she listens.

Sometimes, when she is reading books that have little or no illustration, she likes to augment her own imaginings with what artists have seen; and sometimes, where description does not give a clear picture, it is helpful if we can find paintings correct in detail, and having as well a spirit and atmosphere that convey a feeling of life and imagination. Myths of Greece and Rome; books about people of other days; stories with unfamiliar settings—all of these have much greater importance and reality if the reader has some idea of the appearance of houses and clothes, of the things people used in their homes, and of what they saw around them.

Our collection of prints has grown until we have now a large portfolio stocked with pictures ranging from the Primitives, through the various phases of development in almost all the national schools, and into the modern painters. We have an inexpensive three-panel screen made of some sort of fiber-board of a light buff color. This stands in a corner of the living-room, in a good light, and on it we display "exhibitions" of pictures that illustrate our seasonal interests. Last autumn, when our daughter's school work centered around a study of the Pacific Basin, we mounted on the screen a group of paintings by Gauguin and Rousseau: *Three Tahitians, Ta Matete, The Appeal, Two Tahitian Women, We Greet Thee, Mary* and *An Exotic Landscape*. We enjoyed living with them, and the Gauguins especially, gave us some of the feeling of Polynesian life. Then when The Ballet Russe came to town, and we were planning an expedition to see it, we hung Degas' *The Dancing Girl,* and *La Répétition,* and Laura Knight's *Ballet Girl and Dressmaker,* showing three phases of the life of ballet-dancers. The contrast in style between Degas and Laura Knight stimulated consideration of how two people can see the same sort of thing in an entirely different way.

Pictures of characters and episodes from the Bible are of great interest to us all, and it has been a good study in sociology, to see how a painter's conception of a Biblical subject

could be influenced by the prevailing thought of his time,
and how, through the centuries, religious art has reflected
social and moral philosophies. We have had to explain that
the settings and costumes in most of them are what the
painter saw in his own time, and do not represent the scenes
and garments of Bible days and this, too, is an interesting
point for discussion. Our daughter made one comment that
demonstrated rather amusingly her modern point of view
when we were looking at a print of Giovanni di Paolo's *St.
John the Baptist in the Desert*, with the two figures of St.
John, one just coming out of his house and the other on the
mountain path. She was a little puzzled by it, and then suddenly light broke. "Why," she exclaimed, "that's the beginning of movies!"

A good month before Christmas we begin a series of exhibitions of pictures that have special significance. First of
all, we like to look at our Madonnas, about twenty prints
showing how differently various painters have thought and
felt about the same subject. We hang them in successive
groups, not too many at a time, so that we can really look at
them. Among them are one or two primitives, rich in scarlet
and gold, utterly lifeless, and yet somehow appealing: Cri-
velli's *Madonna and Child*, with its opulent and beautiful
decorative detail, and the central figures quaintly remote
and preoccupied; Bellini's *Madonna and Child in a Landscape*, beautifully warm in color and feeling, Raphael's
Madonna of the Goldfinch, glowing with the beauty of the
color and the affection and sweetness of the mother. Leo-
nardo's *Madonna of the Rocks* is our favorite; the enchant-

ing loveliness of the faces, lit by an unearthly, golden radiance, and the matchless texture and color of background and draperies, give us a deep sense of happiness and satisfaction.

Then, along about the first of December three contrasting pictures of the Annunciation take their places on the screen: Simone Martini's magnificent altarpiece, with its rich detail and sumptuous color; Fra Angelico's fresco, simple, exquisite in color and line, and full of innocent devotion; and the formal yet mystical *Annunciation* of the Master of Moulins.

Jan Steen's *Eve of St. Nicholas* comes out on the sixth of December, to preside over the beginning of our family celebrations, and then after a few days, we return to our illustrations of the Christmas story. Two sets of prints that we especially treasure (both cut from magazines) are Lauren Ford's beautiful paintings of the Ageless Story, with the familiar landscape of New England as the background of the scenes; and a group of paintings by students of the University of Peking, depicting the episodes in the traditional manner of Chinese art, against a Chinese landscape. As our daughter says, "I don't suppose there's another story that painters all over the world have wanted to make pictures for."

After we've lived for a while with our "international Christmas," we put up in their place just one picture, Sassetta's *Journey of the Magi*. This, we know, is chronologically incorrect, but we like to think of the wonderful star beginning to lead the march of events toward Bethlehem, and this picture is so thrilling in its feeling of urgency and gladness that we love to have it where we can see it.

Then comes Christmas Eve, and the screen is garlanded
with greenery. In the center panel we hang the picture that
gathers up all the elements of religious mysticism and pagan
rejoicing—Botticelli's *The Nativity*. This is our picture for
the week of Christmas, and after that there are only three
more: Giotto's *The Flight into Egypt,* Paolo Veronese's *Rest
on the Flight,* and Gerard David's *Rest on the Flight into
Egypt*. These remain until the fifth of January, when Jan
Steen's *Twelfth Night Feast* brings us back to solid earth.

This program is of course subject to change. If we were to
become set in our ways, we should lose the spontaneity of
our enjoyment, and begin to let custom stale our pleasure in
our pictures. A large part of the fun of this kind of thing lies
in catching the interest of the moment at its full flood, and
never laboring any phase of it. Our Christmas exhibitions
have a longer season than most, because Christmas, for us,
is the focal point of the whole year, and because there is
such a wealth of pictures related to it that are good to live
with and so full of meaning and beauty that they can be
looked at year after year without losing their freshness.

The most important thing to us, in our explorations
among great paintings, is to keep our eyes trained to *see,* not
just the pictures themselves, but the beauty and interest of
things around us. Our method has been excitingly successful
with our daughter. She came home from school one windy
day in a glow of pleasure over something she had seen: when
she was walking along toward the little parochial school, a
nun was coming toward her with her habit and veil lifting

and blowing in the wind. The sun was very bright and the sky a deep, rich blue, and the small observer noticed how "everything seemed to be blowing and pointing upward, and my eyes went up too, and saw the gold cross against the blue sky, all among the branches and the gold oak leaves. It was like a lovely picture." Another time we were driving through a green and pleasant stretch of hilly, wooded country. We rounded a curve and came upon a meadow, rising quite sharply in a round green hill. There were a few small whitethorn trees in bloom, and five or six cream colored jersey cows wandering in an irregular line toward the top of the rise. Our passenger in the back seat said, "Oh, look quick! See the lovely design of cows!"

Whether or not our system will be effective with our young man remains to be seen. So far the only pictures in the house that seem to have made any impression on him are the Brangwyn etching of Cannon Street Station, which has a train in it; and a reproduction of *Brahms Seated at the Piano*, at which he points, and asks with a grin, "Is that my father?" But he does enjoy his good picture-books, and if he doesn't want any thing more than that, it will at least do him no harm to have lived with the paintings of the masters.

Yesterday when our daughter came in from school, I had the big portfolio out on the living-room couch, with a great array of pictures spread all around. "Oh, may I look at them before you put them away?" she asked. "Certainly you may. Take as long as you like." I went upstairs to supervise young Duff's bath, and from time to time she would come running up to show me something especially lovely that she had found. When I came down some time later, she was spread-eagled on the living-room floor, looking at the "funnies" in the daily paper. Comic strips can do no harm to a child whose eyes are filled with "images of magnificence."

CHAPTER NINE

"Music My Rampart"[1]

Present mirth hath present laughter,
What's to come is still unsure.

IT was not training for a problematical future, so much
as the capturing of present mirth, that guided our use
of recorded music for the delight of a very small person
when our family was first established as a "going concern."
Her listening life began when she did—how can any parent
not sing to a baby? So we sang, and she listened with that
artless delight that is so endearing in the very young. She
heard records played, too, just because she could not live
with us and not hear them; and it was most interesting to
see a gradually dawning appreciation of the sounds. When
she was eight months old we tried, just for fun, playing
records instead of singing while she sunbathed, and that
was a great success. Graceful melody and well-marked
rhythm brought immediate response, and the tones of various instruments, singly and in combination, became familiar and friendly. By the time she was three she was a
seasoned listener, with definite preferences—always, natu-

[1] From Edna St. Vincent Millay's poems.

109

rally, for uncomplicated forms—and we felt that she was ready to become a collector of her own records. We wanted them to be really her own, in character and appeal as well as in physical possession, and we hit upon the idea of getting as many as possible that "tied up" with the books she knew. This has proved a fine plan, and fully half of her present collection of over forty records have some "literary" association.

She had been brought up on the songs from *The Baby's Opera,* sung both with and without the piano, and we found a nice recording of the tunes, played by violin and piano, very congenial in pitch, tone and tempo, with adequate separation of the airs in the disk so that the needle may be lifted and placed back for re-playing of a particular favorite. This is music that wears well, "Oranges and Lemons," "Upon Paul's Steeple," "There Was a Lady Loved a Swine," and many others, the old familiar tunes from the world's springtime. I have yet to find the child who does not respond with eager delight to the combination of Walter Crane's priceless book and the recorded music. The logical successor to this record, and the ideal introduction to the idea of themes in symphonic music, is Roger Quilter's *The Children's Overture,* which weaves *The Baby's Opera* tunes into a sparkling pattern, beautifully integrated and consistently fresh, spontaneous and thoroughly musical. It is like a Christmas stocking, with one surprise after another popping out of the tinseled wrappings. Of the two available recordings—one played by The New Light Symphony Orchestra under Malcolm Sargent, and the other by the London Philharmonic Orchestra under John Barbirolli—the second seems to have more vitality and is mechanically more accommodated to the child's use, being on one twelve-inch record instead of two ten-inch records as with the former. Children as young as two years, who are familiar with the tunes, will listen entranced to any number of playings, and the whole composition is so skillfully and resourcefully orchestrated that the musically critical grown-up listener finds no weariness in the repetition.

Not so much can be said for the Fraser-Simpson settings of the verses from A. A. Milne's *When We Were Very Young* and *Winnie-the-Pooh*. These have always seemed disappointing in their use of rather obvious melody, and so far as I know, there has been no recording (available in this country, at any rate) with the style and finish of execution necessary to lift them from mediocrity. But it was not part of our plan to impose our own judgment on the young collector, and when she wanted the Milne songs as her next "item," we merely supervised the choosing of the less sloppy of two available recordings. In spite of a regrettable lack of crispness in the articulation of the singer, the songs provided genuine pleasure for the little listener, who quickly learned to "find the places" in her books, and enjoyed the independence of her own program. The interest was not long sustained; for a few weeks we wearily slid down the banisters to breakfast with the king, and writhed over "godda lodda honey on my nice new nose," and then the records found a welcome oblivion. But we cannot say that

the episode was unprofitable: the small person had good
fun, and still sings the songs when she refreshes her memory
of the books. One or two lapses from a standard of excel-
lence, especially where finer composition and performance
are not to be had, will do no harm, and are all a part of
establishing independence of musical judgment, just as the
reading of occasional mediocre books helps to sharpen the
savor of the really sound, satisfying ones that remain in
memory as literary background.

The first story to have its incidental music was *Hansel
and Gretel*, and of all the recordings made of Humperdinck's captivating music, none is more felicitous than the
excerpts sung by *Die Duoptisten*. This anonymous duo
sings in flawlessly clear German, with exquisite tone and all
the spirit and depth demanded by the various moods of
the pieces. The Berlin State Opera Orchestra, under Clemens Schmalstich, provides the accompaniment, and wonderfully exciting performances of "The Witch's Waltz" and
"The Witch's Ride." This little album is a gem for any collection, and I think that few children would outgrow the
pleasure of reading *Hansel and Gretel* with these beautiful
recordings to give a sort of fourth dimension to the reading.

Fairy and folk tales are variously interpreted and told in
music, some successful with little children and some too
sophisticated in style and conception. There is good fun for
the whole family in listening to the various records, and de-
ciding what seems right for the child's feeling for each
story. Except where there is a work of unusual sensitiveness that genuinely conveys a fairy-tale atmosphere, I am

inclined to avoid musical interpretations of fairy tales for a
child's collection. There is enough of the fairy quality in
the works of many of the eighteenth-century composers, for
instance, so that a child who likes to "pair off" a fairy tale
with a musical idea can exercise his own choice and imagination, and this has been found with us a more satisfying
procedure than acceptance of someone else's specified conception of what the tale suggests musically.

Some folk-tale music, such as Sibelius' interpretations of
stories from the *Kalevala*, finds its place in the family collection, accessible to the children if they want to hear it. This
kind of thing requires a much more cultivated ear than the
Hansel and Gretel music, for example, and is usually quite
beyond the enjoyment of the young folk-tale reader, not
only because the musical idiom is too obscure, but also, I
think, because it is a mature interpretation of the socio-
logical implications underlying folklore, rather than the
pure dramatic story element that the child delights in.
Strauss' *Till Eulenspiegel,* on the other hand—used with
Jagendorf's version of the *Merry Pranks*—has all the robust
humor and drollery of the stories, cast in a musical form
thoroughly satisfying to the fun-loving little listener. We
have used, too, folk songs and folk-dance tunes of the various countries from which fairy and folk tales come, and the
understanding that these things are an expression of the
spirit and temperament of the earth's peoples begins to
grow quite naturally, without any self-conscious attempt at
"correlation of social studies." What a happy thing it would
be if "what's to come" for today's children might be shaped

into a comelier aspect by the insight and understanding gained through a knowledge of the real *folk* spirit that shines through music and books.

A modern folk tale, first told in music, is the mirth-provoking *Peter and the Wolf*, in which Sergei Prokofieff catches the authentic flavor of the time-honored tales of his Russian forebears. One of the happiest pictures in a veritable gallery of delightful remembrances of Christmas, 1940, is that of a small girl, perched on the edge of her chair, a dimple playing hide-and-seek in her cheek as she listened to:

Each character of the tale is represented by a corresponding instrument in the orchestra: the bird by a flute, the duck by an oboe, the cat by a clarinet staccato in a low register, the grandfather by a bassoon, the wolf by three horns, Peter by the string quartette, the shooting of the hunters by the kettledrums and the bass drum. Thereby, dear children, you will be able to distinguish the sonorities of the several instruments during the performance of this tale.

Sergei Koussevitsky, in his foreword to Warren Chappell's picture-book, says, "The continued growing interest in *Peter and the Wolf* among adults is especially gratifying to me"; but the work was written especially for children by a composer with extraordinary sympathy and imagination in expressing his musical ideas for their delight, and it seems to me that the proof of his success lies not so much in the appreciation of adults as in the whole-hearted approval of the children who listen time after time with chuckles of pure joy. The combination of Prokofieff's music, the Boston

Symphony Orchestra's performance, and Warren Chappell's pictures is "too much happiness."

The celebration of Christmas, interwoven as it is with the loveliest and most magical of all stories, is incomplete without the use of music to "express the inexpressible." Recorded music never can and never should take the place of singing—singing morning, noon and night, through the whole month of December and on to Twelfth Night. But there is so much that cannot be sung, recordings too numerous even to hint at, of music so glorious and so moving that no child can fail to gather a store of richness for all the year and for all his life from repeated hearings of it. I cannot remember without the quick smart of happy tears, a small, golden-haired girl drowsing in the firelight on Christmas Eve, blissfully drinking in the beauty of *The Shepherds' Christmas Music* from Bach's *Christmas Oratorio*. Corelli's *Christmas Concerto*, too, has a simplicity and an almost wistful gaiety that commends it for use with little children. And I should like to mention one other record, of Jean Planel's exquisitely tender performance of "The Holy Family Resting by the Wayside," from Berlioz' *L'Enfance du Christ*. Here are warmth and gentleness, the intimate human representation of the Holy Family that you find in Veronese's touching picture, *Rest on the Flight*, in which the Christ Baby's tiny nightgown, laid out to dry on a branch of a tree, establishes the kinship of this Family with all the families who through the long years have shared with their precious bairns the celebration of the Holy Child's birthday. It is because of this kinship, and because of the perennial return to pleasure in the imponderables at Christmas time, that the gift of music to a child is richest in its illustration and augmentation of the inexhaustible beauty of the Christmas Story, the most enduring in all our literature.

Next in importance in the literature of the English-speaking peoples are the works of William Shakespeare, and directly a child reaches an age when Lamb's Tales offer a glimpse of joys to come, the lovely settings of the songs from the plays find a ready appeal. "When Daisies Pied," "Where the Bee Sucks," "Hark! Hark! the Lark," "Come Unto These Yellow Sands," these and a host of others, with their beauty of imagery, vitality of language and essentially poetic line, find their way into a child's memory and are fastened there by threads of music more securely than they ever would be if one waited until he were intellectually capable of grasping them through the words alone. Then when the study of the plays as literary units becomes a part of academic work—and the reading of them in a group of contemporaries, under the guidance of a perceptive teacher, is perhaps the most satisfactory approach—happy the child to whom the stories are familiar ground, and for whom the songs leave the limitations of cold print, and live as Shakespeare meant them to, in the warmth of singing voices.

Now I do not mean to suggest that recorded music should ever take the place of the child's own singing and playing, or of music in actual performance. It should be an amplification and an invitation, just as the reading of books enriches and expands experience. The argument, often heard, that a child should not have access to recorded music until he himself has learned to play an instrument seems to me to court rather dangerously the analogy that children should not see the great masterpieces of painting until they themselves have learned to paint. The comment of a sleepy child, going to bed after hearing Elisabeth Schumann's haunting performance of *Der Hirt auf dem Felden* demonstrates the justice of a belief that to hear good music excellently played or sung provides stimulus rather than discouragement: "My head is soaked in music! I must try very hard to learn to sing like that."

It must not be thought, either, that a family's fun in finding music to "illustrate" books should be anything but a casual affair. Pursued consciously as an "educational project," it could defeat its own object of broadening the view. But the natural suggestion—What about "The Moldau"? That is probably the kind of music they played and sang in *Happy Times in Czechoslovakia;* or, Let's play "Sweet Honey-Sucking Bees." Do you remember the bit where Master Skylark sang a song that was part of a madrigal?— often kindles a spark of response. And if it does not, for the moment, neither book nor music is spoiled by the forcing of interest.

The whole use of music with books grows out of a genuine and spontaneous feeling for both, and is given substance by eagerness and resource. It is only natural that parents whose love of music has brought deep and abiding joy should pass along the keys of the kingdom to those who must take, along with the sweets of man's achievement, the bitter fruits of his failure to hold fast to that which is good. The parent's job at best is one subject to constant bewilderment and dismay; but if he can give to his child not only gifts of character, but the gift of belief in the goodness of the human spirit as it shines so serenely and steadily in the creation of enduring beauty, then surely no effort is lost. By whatever means come readiest, children should be led into the enjoyment of pleasures that age cannot wither nor custom stale. And if the family's temperament and inclination make the use of music with books a congenial pursuit, the very means becomes a source of endless delight, and establishes a bond that grows in strength and sweetness as the years go by.

CHAPTER TEN

"These Thy Mercies"

B READ-MAKING is an occupation very conducive, I find, to reflective contemplation. Bread is so fundamental, and there is such satisfaction in kneading and shaping the responsive sponge, and in taking the finished loaves, brown and comely and sweet-smelling, from the oven. I have found myself, on every baking day this winter, thinking about the wise grandfather in Monica Shannon's *Dobry,* who said:

"When we eat the good bread, we are eating months of sunlight, weeks of rain and snow from the sky, richness out of the earth. We should be great, each of us radiant, full of music and full of stories. Able to run the way clouds do, able to dance like the snow and the rain. But nobody takes time to think that he eats all these things and that sun, rain, snow are all a part of himself."

I have thought how strange it is that in a world full of hunger, we should be able to have our good food every day; and how great is the responsibility of all of us who are fed, to value what we eat, and to enjoy it with a whole-hearted pleasure. I have thought about a funny little incident that happened several years ago, when I was teaching nursery-school. It was a lovely spring morning, and all the children were bursting with high spirits. One little girl, usually very quiet and rather repressed, came bouncing out of her mother's car, shouting, "Guess what I had for breakfast this morning?" A whole catalogue sprang to my lips of absurd and appetizing delicacies suitable for breaking the fast on such a morning. But the words froze when her mother said reprovingly, "Mary dear, don't you remember? It's rude to talk about food." "Now what's all this nonsense?" I wondered. I have turned it over in my mind from time to time ever since; was it our Puritan ancestors' horror of the sin of gluttony, surviving in a stilted social convention? What a pity, I have thought this winter, that a little girl's pleasure in her good breakfast should be spoiled by such an artificial stricture. Why, when you think of all the children who have never had enough to eat, and who could not even imagine such food as we accept as a matter of course, it is worse than rude *not* to talk about food—it is downright ungrateful!

Some of the best conversations that I have ever heard have been all about food, and there is a special warmth and intimacy about books in which the details of eating and drinking are described with a proper regard for their importance. Hunger, and the satisfaction of hunger are almost the least common denominator of human living, and the fact is recognized in the very first literature that children know. Count the nursery rhymes that are concerned with it: the Queen in her parlor, eating bread and honey; poor wistful Simon going without his pie because he had no penny; Jack Horner, hooking plums out of his pie with an exploratory thumb; Curly-locks feeding upon strawberries, sugar and cream. There are white bread, brown bread and plum cake for the Lion and the Unicorn; hot boiled beans and very good butter for ladies and gentlemen; cakes and wine for Jenny Wren.

Then you remember the tempting meals in Beatrix Potter's books—Peter Rabbit indulging in illicit greens in Mr. MacGregor's garden, and his sisters supping royally on bread and milk and blackberries. Jeremy Fisher's dinner of roast grasshopper with ladybird sauce has quite an epicurean sound, and the tea-party in "The Pie and the Patty-pan" makes your mouth water: "the pie proved extremely toothsome, and the muffins were light and hot."

When I ask our four-year-old what he would like for Sunday breakfast, he says "Get some flour and eggs and milk and sugar and butter, and make a plate of most lovely pancakes. Fry them in butter made out of melted tigers, and they'll be just as yellow and brown as little tigers." So they are, and how much more we enjoy them than we should if they were just ordinary pancakes.

There is real value in a child's enjoyment of food in books. In the first place, it adds to his pleasure in his own food, by appetizing association. It stimulates his curiosity about unfamiliar foods, and he is predisposed to like them when he knows that his friends in books have enjoyed them. This may seem a rather mundane consideration, but I feel that any child who approaches food with caution is handicapped. He loses the zest of mealtimes, and cuts himself off from the normal hearty delight in things to eat that is surely a part of living with gusto.

Then there is another interesting thing that I have discovered about talk of food in the books that children read. Ever since our daughter began to read on her own, we have observed that the books about real life that have made the deepest impression on her have been the ones in which food plays a very definite part. Children understand about eating; it is a sort of touchstone by which they can judge the economic and social status of the people they read about, and to a great extent, their character and resourcefulness as well. The plentifulness or scarcity of food, and the kinds of food and ways of eating it are concrete and easily understood indexes to conditions and circumstances that would not make sense to them, stated in any other terms.

Ruth Sawyer's *Roller Skates* is a gorgeous book, witty and wise, and packed with the excitement of just *being*. Here you find an exuberant delight in food, every meal described with honest pleasure, and a fine care in pointing up contrasts. When Lucinda goes on a picnic with Tony, his contribution is fruit from his father's fruit-stand, and potatoes roasted in tin cans; hers, meat sandwiches and jelly sandwiches and cup-cakes. She goes to tea at the Gilligan's, and revels in the simple, hearty food: ham and Irish potatoes, gooseberry jam and griddle-bread "cut pie-ways and eaten hot off the griddle with lots of butter." Then at Thanksgiving dinner at Aunt Ellin's there was "a vile mess called terrapin, and fish to fiddle with. . . . For her part, she kept empty, deliberately empty for turkey and dessert." Our daughter was nine years old when she read *Roller Skates,* and she understood perfectly how potatoes roasted in tin cans belong to a different social and economic level from terrapin and turkey, but Ruth Sawyer took care that there should be no prejudice against either, except by reason of a child's preference for simple food.

We remember two wonderful breakfasts that typify security and comfort of two different kinds. In Charlie May Simon's *Bright Morning* on the day the family were moving to a smaller house

. . . the coffeepot sang and bubbled in the ashes, and a pan of oatmeal stood steaming on the warm hearth, smelling of its goodness . . . The parents ate at the parlor table, and the children sat on the floor around the fire on the rolled carpet holding their bowls of oatmeal in their laps. Never had a breakfast tasted so good before. Even Anna felt the excitement of moving-day, as she toasted bread enough for all, over the hot coals, and spread it with butter and jam.

Our daughter loves the feeling of that because it reminds her of our own moving-day breakfasts in front of the fire on the frosty September mornings when we leave our cottage to come home to the sedateness of "civilized meals."

Breakfast in *Those Plummer Children* is a much more dignified affair, and the menu bespeaks a casual southern opulence that the nice family in *Bright Morning* have never known: "sausages, fried apples in ruddy rings, spoonbread and poached eggs and strawberry jam." At the other end of the scale is the humble hominy, that Peter Pocket and his grandmother made, in May Justus' story of life in the Tennessee Mountains. But hominy is ambrosia, when you are really hungry, and our daughter realized, when she read about it, that hunger is the best sauce for any food.

Not very long ago I was deputed to fetch books from the public library for the whole family, and I found myself not quite able to remember whether or not our First Reader had ever had "A Candle in the Mist." But it looked attractive so I brought it along. "Does this look familiar?" I asked her. She looked at it consideringly for a moment and then said "Oh yes, I'm so glad you brought it! This is the one that has Janey's bee-autiful birthday supper in it." She ruffled through the pages and read: "A swirl of snowy potato, scooped out where melted butter made a golden lake. Pink ham with cream gravy, sour-cream biscuits, feather-light within, crispy-crusty without, buckwheat honey, dark but delicious." She looked up with a comical expression of pain. "Doesn't it just make you *groan* with hunger?"

Another favorite "food book" is *Tag-along Tooloo*. We could do with a little more about the crab-catching expedition and the supper that followed, though there is a volume of description in Melaynay's "Come on now and get yo' bread and butter. Dat's all we got to go wid 'em. Ain't no sense in cluttering up your innards wid anything else when you got crab-meat." But nothing is left to the imagination except blissful gormandizing when the Christmas Eve party comes along. I marvel at the household that could supply such a feast at short notice:

There were bowls of stuffed dates frosted with sugar; plates of
raisins and figs; snowy piles of sugared pecans and candied
orange-peel; little china dishes filled with salted nuts, and
baskets of almonds, walnuts, Brazil nuts and filberts in their
shells. There were silver platters full of dark, spiced cookies,
bursting their sides with nuts and citron; and rich, wine-moist
fruitcake, smelling like perfume. There were oranges and apples, and plates of many-colored candies; hard candy and chocolate creams, and pink and lavender bonbons with little sugared
flowers on top.

Louisa May Alcott's "Candyland" pales into insignifi-
cance by comparison with that banquet of sweetness!

This is all in the lavish tradition of American hospitality,
which has a long history behind it. Books about the early
days describe over and over again the eagerness to share
whatever the household could offer. Our forebears had a
simple pleasure in good food, as well they might when so
often it was a matter of grim struggle to get it. When our
daughter read in *Away Goes Sally* about the bounteous,
satisfying food, she decided that "pioneer life couldn't
have been so bad." The provisions that went out to the hay-
makers suggest no shadow of want:

Baked beans, corned beef, mince pie, doughnuts, plumcake
which the aunts had packed with last year's perry, a sort of
cider made from their own pears, and a jug of Jamaica.

And what graciousness and ease are reflected in Sally's
preparations for tea,

She raked the hot embers into six mounds, and put on six iron pots: coffee for Uncle Joseph, chocolate for Uncle Eben who loved sweets, strong old Hyson tea for Aunt Nannie, weak Hyson for Aunt Deborah and souchong for Aunt Esther. Sally had a little pot of her own . . . so she too had her own chocolate like Uncle Eben's but with more milk in it. While the water was boiling she spread the table, made cream toast, and laid out a loaf of new bread, a big pat of butter, gooseberry preserves, apple and cherry pie and doughnuts.

But this, after all, was in New England, in the early nineteenth century, years after the Pilgrims had waged their bitter battle with hunger and cold and disease. *Away Goes Sally* is a picture of their triumph against the cruel unfriendliness of a new land. Move westward, however, and even as little time ago as seventy years, there was a story to tell of pioneer privations and resourcefulness. Few books have provided more sheer excitement for our daughter than Laura Ingalls Wilder's stories of homesteading, first in Wisconsin, then in Indian territory, then still farther west, in Dakota. Here, indeed, are "books that shall be classic for the young." Courage, humor, resourcefulness and an unbreakable endurance flow in a strong undercurrent through all these accounts of adjustment to a series of new and difficult circumstances, and food is here again the index to the ups and downs of prosperity. It is no longer just an element of pleasure and gracious occasions; it is a constant, fundamental need. When food is scarce, you share anxiety and suffering with the gallant family, and when it is plentiful their deep thankfulness somehow becomes your own. What they had to eat, and the circumstances in which they ate it, are described in faithful detail, and they are important and revealing to the reader because meals eaten seventy years ago are still, to the writer, a matter of vital consequence. How unforgettable is the occasion in *On the Banks of Plum Creek,* when Pa made his winter expedition to town and was lost in the blizzard. The family waiting at home in the terror of the howling wind and the bitter cold, ate their frugal meal of beans and fresh bread, seasoned with the bitter salt of apprehension. Then miraculously Pa came home after a night spent buried under a snowdrift.

Ma quickly warmed some of the bean-broth and gave it to him. "That's good," he said. "That warms a fellow." [After he has told the story of his adventure—funny, now that it is safely over—he produces a] "flat square-edge can of bright tin." "What do you think I have brought you for Christmas dinner? . . . Oysters! Nice fresh oysters! . . . I ate up the oyster crackers and I ate up the Christmas candy, but by jinks," said Pa, "I brought the oysters home."

. . . The dishes made small clinking sounds as Mary set the table. Carrie rocked herself in the rocking-chair and Ma went gently between the table and the stove. In the middle of the table she set a milk-pan full of beautiful brown baked beans, and now from the oven she took the square baking-pan full of golden corn-bread. The rich brown smell and the sweet golden smell curled deliciously together in the air . . . Everything was so good. Grasshoppers were gone, and next year Pa could harvest the wheat. Tomorrow was Christmas, with oyster stew for dinner.

The next Christmas was better. Mr. and Mrs. Boast came unexpectedly, struggling for miles through wind and snow, to share it with them.

Laura helped Ma set on the big platter of golden, fried mush, a plate of hot biscuits, a dish of fried potatoes, a bowl of codfish gravy and a glass dish full of dried apple sauce. "I'm sorry we have no butter," said Ma. "Our cow gives so little milk we can't make butter any more." . . . "Such a breakfast as that, like Christmas came only once a year." And what a dinner! Before Pa, on the big platter, lay the huge roasted rabbit with piles of bread and onion stuffing steaming around it. From a dish on one side stood up a mound of mashed potatoes, and on the other side stood a bowl of rich brown gravy. There were plates of hot Johnny cake and of small hot biscuits. There was a dish of cucumber pickles.

The year after that was *The Long Winter.*

There was no more coal in town. The kerosene was low in the lamp though Ma lighted it only while they ate supper. There would be no more meat until the train came. There was no butter and only a little fat-meat dripping was left to spread on the bread. There were still potatoes, but no more than flour enough for one more bread-making. But Pa said, "We will have to contrive. We'll manage it! Needs must, when the devil drives."

And they did manage it. There was oyster soup for Christmas dinner, "good, even though the milk was mostly water," and everybody had presents. Our daughter remarked that it sounded awfully like the March girls' Christmas, that dreadful winter when their father was away at the war. "Isn't it fun, the way families can make Christmas out of almost nothing, when they love Christmas and love each other?"

One of the most memorable meals in the saga of the Ingalls family is the dinner of blackbird pie, in *Little Town on the Prairie,* during the heart-breaking summer when the blackbirds destroyed the grain.

Pa cut into the pie's crust with a big spoon, and turned over a big chunk of it onto a plate. The underside was steamed and fluffy. Over it he poured spoonfuls of thin brown gravy, and beside it he laid half a blackbird, browned and so tender that the meat was slipping from the bones. . . . They all agreed that blackbird pie was even better than chicken pie. There were, besides, new potatoes and peas, and sliced cucumbers, and young boiled carrots that Ma had thinned from the rows, and creamy cottage cheese. And the day was not even Sunday. As long as the blackbirds lasted, and the garden was green, they could eat like this every day.

What a shining tradition we inherit from the pioneers, who flavored their lean meals with fortitude and imagination, and their fat meals with thankfulness and enjoyment! Today's children find their pride in it through books like Laura Ingalls Wilder's, written with zest and affection and a true sense of proportion.

America has another tradition, of food brought from other countries, and preserved in kitchens all over the United States, where the lore of the Old World is translated by the skill and resourcefulness of "new American" cooks into meals of a surpassing savoriness. One of the first books to introduce the idea of foreign ways of cooking to American children is Margery Clark's *The Poppy Seed Cakes*. This jolly tale is simple and amusing, on just the right scale for little people who would be baffled by talk of elaborate grown-up food, but are enchanted by the dear little cakes that Andrewshek's Auntie Katushka made for him, and sprinkled with the poppy seeds that she had brought from the old country. Our young son is waiting for the day when his mother will get round to making poppy seed cakes for him.

Our daughter's fancy turns to Italian food, which is not surprising to anyone who has read Valenti Angelo's books. What meals the Santo family sat down to, in *Hill of Little Miracles*—

The group shouted with joy when a huge platter of rice, cooked to a golden brown in a rich sauce of olive oil, mushrooms, tomatoes, chopped onions and chicken livers, was brought in. Soon after that, a large round platter of *fritto misto*, a mixture of chicken, zucchini, celery, young artichokes, eggplant, all fried in egg batter, took the place of honor on the table. So Patrick stayed a little longer, just to praise Mamma Santo's *fritto misto*. Incidentally he washed the *fritto misto* down with another glass of zinfandel.

The wedding dinner is a feast to remember.

The food made everyone happy, and the house was alive with friendliness. [There was minestrone soup, thick and savory; then] the ravioli were brought in, two huge platters of paste stuffed with chicken meat and vegetables. The delicious odor of the grated cheese mixed with the rich sauce made the guests forget the soup they had eaten. . . . Presently Flora helped her mother carry in two huge earthen bowls filled with *chiopino*, a mixture of steamed clams, crab legs and large shrimps swimming in a sauce of olive oil seasoned with chopped garlic and parsley.

Compare those meals with what you read of the pitiful scarcity of good food in Italy nowadays, and the phrase "Freedom from Want" has a stronger impact. I think it is a legitimate illustration for children of the contrast between life here and in other parts of the world.

We have had great fun with books that tell about the daily food of other countries. British food is familiar to our daughter, but she loves to read about the "piles of bread and butter, crumpets, coconut cakes and a large cake with pink icing," when Jane and Michael go to tea with Mary Poppins' uncle, Mr. Wigg. Everything from porridge to pemmican in Arthur Ransome's books sounds good, and what the Bastable children have to eat and drink is so delightfully and unmistakably English—pastries and sausage rolls, ginger beer, roast chestnuts, roast mutton, tea-cake and herrings—that the very names make us hungry and homesick. And how we have laughed over *The Family from One End Street*, with "sardines and chocolate biscuits for tea to celebrate," for we all have a passion for those chocolate biscuits done up in tinsel paper.

We once met on board ship three schoolteachers from a town in Quebec, who were going to spend the summer in

Europe. We thought how they would enjoy visiting in France, the home of their ancestors, and looked forward to seeing them on the homeward trip. But what a disappointment it was; to judge from their conversation, their whole holiday had been a succession of disagreeable encounters with outlandish food. In France they had been given queer greens to eat, sorrel and the like, and in Italy, fish appeared on the table complete with heads. What a pity that they had never had the sort of books that our book-traveler reads! She knows, from reading, about the thrifty French use of sorrel and dandelion leaves for greens. Hector Malot makes them sound delicious in *Nobody's Girl,* when Perrine contrives a supper of ducks' eggs, fish from the brook, sorrel soup and wild gooseberries for her friend Rosalie. There is wholesome peasant food in René Bazin's *Juniper Farm,* and the more sophisticated food in Marjorie Fischer's *Street Fair* is typically French, and so enticing: the hors d'oeuvres, small dark olives, quartered hard-boiled eggs with mayonnaise, sliced tomatoes, sardines, anchovies, sliced beets, quartered hearts of artichoke, tuna fish, radishes, rice with peppers, slices of sausages "with bright colored odors." And even better than hors d'oeuvres, according to Anna, was the *bouillabaisse;* John agreed solemnly "It's the best thing I ever in my whole life ate!"

When you read about people heartily enjoying food you've never heard of before, you are not likely to be dismayed by boiled sorrel in vinegar and oil, or fish with the heads on. Our child has done a sort of Gourmet's Grand Tour of Europe, and tells with reminiscent delight of the food she has eaten by proxy. *Happy Times in Czechoslovakia* were all celebrated with food: The Christmas Eve supper of mushroom soup, fish and black gravy with prunes, dumplings, and cooked farina flavored with honey, butter and ginger; the Harvest Festival feast of young goose, dumplings, cabbage kolachy, and many other goodies; and the Easter *butchta,* round coffee cakes filled with cheese, prune jam or poppy seed, that were taken to church to be blessed. How right it seems to her, that food and festival should be synonymous.

She likes the strange names of things, and the unfamiliar combinations of ingredients; she likes to be allowed into the kitchen, to see how food is prepared. " 'Meat rolled in cabbage leaves. There is nothing that tastes better,' said Masha, when the grandmother pulled from out the oven the steaming pot"; and our gourmet leans over grandmother's shoulder, to see how it looks and smells. In *Kobi, a Boy of Switzerland* she makes the acquaintance of potatoes fried with caraway seeds, honey-cake, sausage and onions; and she watches the cheese being made by Kobi's grandfather. She tastes wild boar and wonderful home-brewed beer on a Norwegian farm. Best of all is the life with food in *Dobry,* for here she sees the seed time and the harvest, and eats the good bread that goes into the oven with Roda's prayer, "God, please bless this bread and each person who eats of it. Bad luck blow away like chaff on the wind, good luck stay with us." She is "warmed to red inside" with the first tomatoes of the year, dug out from under the snow where they are preserved after the Bulgarian custom, and

eaten by moonlight. "Crisp, too, juicy and really cold. Perfect!" There is food for the spirit, too, in *Dobry*, wholesome and sustaining, and as simple and good as Roda's
bread.

She travels in farther-off countries, too, where the climate
produces foods still less familiar than the European ones.
She learns from *Boomba Lives in Africa* that "African food
is good. And Boomba's mother had prepared a good dinner
of white rice which she put in a bowl. Upon the rice was
tapioca-leaf spinach and four small fishes. . . . This very
good food was seasoned with gold-colored pepper. And over
this food Boomba's mother had poured palm-oil." She
learns from *Totaram* a little about Indian food, "goat's flesh
and vegetables, cooked swimming in oil with handfuls of
chilies." There is a beautiful description in *The Moon's
Birthday* of the Chinese ceremonies in celebration of the
kitchen-god, whose paper image is placed upon a paper
horse, and given money for his journey to the place where
Ancestors dwell; then he is set afire, and the paper ash flies
upward, taking messages from the family to the Ancestors.
There is a feast in the god's honor, "golden persimmons on
a round blue plate" and rice flour balls, with sugar and
spice in the middle that comes out like sirup when you
bite into them. *Little Pear* has delicious Chinese food in it:
tang hulurs made of red fruits, eight or ten on a stick, all
covered with candied sirup; steamed dumplings stuffed
with cabbage and bean sauce; and when little Pear comes
in, cold and ravenous after flying his kite in the wind, there

is "a very large supper of fried cornmeal, beansprouts and hot tea."

All these glimpses into the fundamental ways of domestic life in other countries are a warm invitation to understanding of ways different from our own. Once you have broken bread with people, even if it is only in a book, you are less likely to be intolerant of their customs and beliefs.

Just as food in books has proved, with us, a fine means of coming to know people, so it has been a stimulus to learning about the sources of food, and its uses and values. I think children miss a great part of the simple pleasure of home life if the kitchen is an unfamiliar department. To me, a child who has never licked the bowls after the cake mixing has never really lived. Our two hang about while the cooking is going on, like bees around a honey-pot, and we talk about the importance of this or that kind of food, what it does for our bodies, and how it should be prepared to preserve its full value. We talk about where various things come from, rice and tapioca, sugar, tea, bananas, pineapples and so on. We have found several books to instruct us in these matters. Even our youngest member has his two favorite food books: Janet Smalley's *Rice to Rice Pudding* tells, after the manner of "this is the house that Jack built," about many things familiar to every child, like rice and butter, peanuts, ham, salmon, and honey; and the pictures that help the stories along are full of fun and activity. The Petershams' *The Story Book of Food* is more advanced, but the language is simple and lively and the pictures full of color and interest, so that even at the tender age of four, our son finds it appealing and understandable.

Quite lately we have found two books that seem to us as exciting as fiction. Ruth Orton Camp's *The Story of Markets* provides a fine background for exploration of the sources of food. It tells the history of trading in foods from "almost as far back as the earliest knowledge we have of man," right down to the development of our modern chain-store markets, with all sorts of fascinating details about the countries where foods grow, and the things that people eat and have eaten in various times and places. There is a perfectly astonishing list of the foods served at a single banquet in ancient Rome, beginning with olives, dormice and wild honey, and ending up, after forty other sweets and savories, with thrushes in pastry stuffed with nuts, quinces, oysters and scallops. Our daughter gave a whoop when she read it—"So that's why Rome fell! Tummyache!"

Our other book is a volume for the connoisseur of books as well as of foods. *Spice on the Wind* describes the importance of spice in history—"One can think of spice almost as a milestone marking the growth of civilization in one ancient land after another"—and tells how and when various spices were found, how they are grown, harvested, packed and prepared for market, and how they are used in cooking. Pepper, cloves, vanilla, nutmeg, ginger and cinnamon has each a chapter to itself; and at the end is a chapter on various other spices and herbs, like anise and basil, cayenne, chervil, coriander, fennel, rosemary, saffron, tarragon and thyme, whose very names are enticing.

These books bring geography right to our dinner-table, in a manner both stimulating and romantic. And, rather interestingly, we have found in this sort of geography a way of giving our ten-year-old an intelligent understanding of one of the ways in which the war affects our very own world. We do not believe that you can or should shut children away from the realities of these times; but we do believe that whatever of the war they share must be on their own level of experience and comprehension. Otherwise they will be the prey of fear of what they do not understand, and of the tendency to unbuttoned emotionalism that seizes people in time of war. Our daughter is medium intelligent; she reads the newspaper, and hears snatches of war news from the radio, so she knows what is going on; and a rather too vivid and sensitive imagination has given her some bad times. We have neither the right nor the means to protect her from the hurt of knowing that people are suffering, but we can direct her concern with the war toward those phases of it that she can understand. We welcome the chance that our altered food supply provided to let her share in a healthy, normal fashion the domestic problems that arise.

It has all happened quite casually. The first time we asked for bananas at the grocer's, and were told that there weren't any, and wouldn't be any for some time, she wanted to know why. We told her about where bananas come from, and about the difficulties of shipping. She was tremendously interested, and asked what other foods might become scarce for the same reason. Out came the atlas, to show her the seaways that ships follow, in normal times, to bring various foods to this country, and it was astonishing to find how much could be learned about the war without once touching on matters too grave for a ten-year-old to be troubled with. Gradually, as she grows older, we can deal with the reasons why war brings famine, and why our world must be reorganized so that all people shall have a share in its bounty. When that time comes, she will be ready to think intelligently about these things, for through her reading she has developed an interest and pleasure in food, knowledge of its properties and varying character, and sympathy with the folk who eat it.

CHAPTER ELEVEN

"Of Brooks, of Blossoms, Birds and Bowers"

WHEN our small daughter was four years old, a visitor, seeing her one afternoon absorbed in play with a multitude of paper dolls, asked, "Is that your hobby?" "Oh, no," she replied, "it's just a thing I do."

That is an apt way of describing most of the interests we follow in this family. We have none of the single-mindedness of direction that turns liking for a thing into particularized, exclusive concern with it. We have, rather, a steady glow of pleasure in a great variety of things, a sort of "all's grist that comes to the mill" attitude, which if it gives us no great authority on any one subject, keeps us constantly on the bubble with quiet excitement.

We are not, for instance, either very methodical or very scientific in our study of natural history. It is "just a thing we do" because we live all the year round close to the infinite variety and surprise of natural things. We spend our summers in the woods and by the waters of Georgian Bay, and autumn, winter and spring at the edge of a middle-western town, where birds, squirrels and rabbits live among our oak trees, and wild flowers come poking their heads up in our lawn and flower-beds. We like to know the names and characteristics of birds, animals, flowers, trees and stars, so that we can recognize and talk about them. But we care more about how a black-and-white warbler looks playing about in a rain-spangled honeysuckle bush, than about being able to describe all the scientific details of its wing structure. We take no competitive pride in reporting the earliest-known arrival of the scarlet tanager; just so long as we see the flash of his scarlet wings in the woodlot on any spring day, we are quite content.

The books that have provided us with a working basis of information for intelligent observation of things out-of-doors are not concerned with the intricacies of botanical, entomological or zoological detail any more than is necessary for accuracy. We use field books for birds, flowers, trees and the stars. Chester Reed's *The Flower Guide* is a nice compact little volume that fits into a pocket to go on all our walks in the northern woods. Each flower has a picture in color, simple and clear, and the index is arranged according to color. The descriptive text is nicely written, and gives just the information we need to identify any unfamiliar flower or plant that we meet. *Land Birds East of the Rockies* is an equally good companion, in constant use all the spring, when it lives with the bird-glasses on our dining-room window-sill, so that we can quickly discover the names of any strangers that appear during mealtimes on the bird-tray or in the woodlot; and in the summer when it stays on our cottage veranda, ready for work if a new bird flies to the pine trees. *Water Birds East of the Rockies* goes with us in the boat on all summer expeditions and helps us to make friends with the flocks of birds that live on the outer islands.

For identifying unfamiliar trees both in Illinois and Georgian Bay, we use Carlton Curtis' *A Guide to the Trees*, which uses the leaf as the principal means of identification. We supplement this with a fine large illustrated pamphlet published by the Canadian Government, which gives particularly good information about the various kinds of evergreens so characteristic of the growth on our rocky, wind-swept islands. This booklet is unhappily no longer available, so we cherish our dog-eared copy.

We find William Tyler Olcott's *Field Book of the Stars* the most satisfactory for our study of the sky. A large diagram showing the appearance and relative positions of stars and constellations on the first night of each quarter precedes each season's work, and provides a quick and easy means of identifying any star under observation. We try to "photograph" these diagrams in our minds, so that when we go out to lie on the rocks at night we shall be able to enjoy just looking, but it is quite possible with the help of a flashlight to make use of the maps for settling doubt about the identity of any particular star.

Mosses and ferns carpet the ground in the deep northern woods where we go exploring, and these (especially the mosses) are a fascinating study of "perfection in littleness." Herbert Durand's *The Field Book of Common Ferns* is very satisfactory for identifying most ferns that we come across; so far it has failed us only once, when we happened on an exquisite little rock fern so unusual that only one of the ardent botanists of our acquaintance had ever seen it before. He told us its many-syllabled name, which we promptly forgot. It remains quite as beautiful by our Indian-sounding designation, "Little rock fern that curls up in the heat."

The only guide to mosses that we have found, E. M. Dunham's *How to Know the Mosses*, falls short of perfection because of its lack of good illustrations. We have to carry our specimens back to the house and take a good deal of time to determine, from descriptions, the names of the enchanting green stars, whorls and spirals that grow so profusely all among the tree roots. But it is worth the trouble. As our daughter says, some people are more difficult to make friends with than others, but the ones you take the most trouble with are often the most satisfactory.

We have never discovered a book on geology simple enough and sufficiently pertinent to the kind of thing we need to know, for our ten-year-old to use with any profit. This is rather a pity, for the rock formations and the evidences of glacial and volcanic action in our Georgian Bay islands are impressive and exciting. A little later on we shall be able to read Enos Mill's *The Romance of Geology* and one or two other books of that sort, but in the meantime we are anxious not to spoil her interest by urging books that are too mature, so we just supply what information we can from our own knowledge of geology, and fill in the gaps by asking questions in the right places.

The butterflies, moths and various other insects that we see are almost all known to us just from having heard their names all our lives. But when we come across something unfamiliar we consult various books in the public library— W. J. Holland's *The Butterfly Book* and H. J. Comstock's *Insect Life: An Introduction to Nature Study* together cover the field pretty thoroughly. This usually means remembering until the autumn the appearance and behavior of insects we have seen in the summer, which is a rather chanceful method of procedure. But if any insect interests us enough to make us want to know its name we watch it so attentively that our memory is likely to be reasonably accurate. We hope that one of these days we shall be able to add these two rather expensive books to our cottage library, but in the meantime the cultivation of accurate visual memory is a useful exercise for both children and grownups.

We seldom read books on Natural History just for fun. Our own life with live and growing things is so satisfying and exciting that except where a book provides information, or is apart from its subject a fine piece of literature (parts of George Gissing's *The Private Papers of Henry Ryecroft* and of W. N. P. Barbellion's *The Journal of a Disappointed Man* have this distinction, for grown-ups) it is likely to seem a "pleasure twice removed." The books we do love are the ones that reflect a discerning pleasure in the beauty and perennial wonder of the natural world. When we find in something we are reading a passage that describes a thing familiar and delightful to us, we say, "Oh, he noticed

that too!" and feel a rush of affection for the "friend unseen, unknown" who wrote down his pleasure for us to
enjoy.

Sometimes a thing newly seen brings back the memory of
prose or poetry that catches the special quality of that thing
with point and grace. Then we see it more attentively because of knowing that other eyes have carried a message of
its importance to a mind much like our own, but more
articulate.

We especially value Beatrix Potter's books for the feeling
of warm pleasure in the beauties of the English countryside
that shines through both pictures and stories. Take *The
Tale of Mr. Tod,* a tale of action if ever there was one. But
all through it you find the sights and sounds and smells that
are perceived only by someone who knows and loves the
country: a "sea of blue hyacinths" in the wood, the smell of
fresh earth, the harsh cry of a jay; and as the sun came up,
"in the valley there was a sea of white mist, with the golden
tops of the trees showing through." *The Fairy Caravan* is
full of the loveliness and peace of rural England, and in
almost all of the Peter Rabbit books there are little glimpses
of field and wood that have the quality of sunshine.

Beatrix Potter's animals, human though they are in their
behavior, have still the essential characteristics of their kind
as they appear in their relationship with the human world.
Rabbits invade and plunder gardens, squirrels are mis-
chievous and quarrelsome, but their gentle hearts and soft
furry bodies secure them indulgence and affection. On the
other hand, foxes are disagreeable, predatory individuals,

badgers dirty and slow, rats vicious and dishonest, and they deserve—and get—no love at all. Beatrix Potter is never sentimental about her animal characters; her manner of presenting them is as brisk, humorous and penetrating as Jane Austen's way with human folk. Children who make acquaintance with the animal kingdom by way of Miss Potter's books see live creatures as familiar friends. Any wild bunny in the woodlot may be Peter Rabbit or one of his numerous kinfolk. The gray squirrel that lands with a thud on the feeding-tray is welcomed joyously as Timmy Tiptoes. Even the ungainly porcupine that comes blundering through the woods is regarded with a certain affection because she is second-cousin-twice-removed to Mrs. Tiggywinkle.

The Wind in the Willows is another book that has the pervasive charm of deep, instinctive affection for the loveliness of the natural world. The coming of day and the mystery of night, the swing of the year through its seasons, the intimate beauties of meadow, hedgerow and copse are all things of great importance to Kenneth Grahame. He never dwells on them at the expense of his story; they are simply so much a part of it that the reader somehow feels that is all a part of himself, something that he has seen with delight and remembered with joy. The animals who people Mr. Grahame's pages are richly and lovably human, and their dwellings are gloriously imagined. Yet you learn in some subtle fashion a great deal about the natural ways and habitats of wild folk. After we had read the book one summer, our daughter summed up her feeling for it with, "Well, all I can say is, there is simply nothing half so worth doing as reading *The Wind in the Willows*."

Then there is Felix Salten's *Bambi,* of which John Galsworthy said, "For delicacy of perception and essential truth, I hardly know any story of animals that can stand beside this life study of a forest deer." Every page of it is instinct with deep respect and tenderness for wild creatures, and understanding knowledge of their ways. It is written with a strong sense of the beauties, large and little, of the forest world, and conveys a feeling of their value and permanence. We were of two minds about putting it into the hands of a sensitive ten-year-old, for there are moments in it of genuine tragedy. But we were reluctant to have her see the film version of the story without first giving her a chance at the original. We told her by way of preparation, that things happen in the book just exactly as they do in the life of animals, and that if it sometimes seemed harsh and sad, she must remember that Nature can be cruel as well as kind, and that she is always just. We explained how this is so, and then left her to her reading. We need not have worried about how the book would affect her; when she had finished it she sighed. "It's so funny and nice in spots," she said, "and sometimes it almost made me cry. But it's sort of *complete,* isn't it?"

Our small boy has his favorite "nature book" too, Virginia Lee Burton's *The Little House.* Both drama and beauty are in the pictures that show the rising up and the going down of the sun, the waxing and waning of the moon, and the changing colors of the countryside as the seasons turn. The text that describes them is simple and rather poetic; you feel that the author really values these things. And the boy who owns the book sees moon and stars, snowflakes and apple blossoms and flying autumn leaves with perception sharpened because they have been shown to him, with affection and beauty, in a book.

There is no end to the poetry that celebrates the enchantment of natural things. Just to be able to remember and speak it at the right moment seems to add a special beauty to the things we see, because a poet has his own special way of seeing and interpreting. Our children have heard a great deal of the poetry of nature; we say it, whether they will understand it or not, because we can't help it, and probably wouldn't if we could. It finds a safe repository, that I know. For the cherry trees came into bloom a few days ago, and our daughter came in with a cluster of blossoms pinned over each ear, "Just *smell* me!" she said ecstatically. And then, "I've been trying all the way home to remember that poem that you say about the cherry trees. Tell it to me." So I told her "Loveliest of trees, the cherry now" and I suspect there was a quaver in my voice,

> "Since to look at things in bloom
> Fifty years is little room,"

and the loveliest thing I know is the blossoming spirit of a girl "rising ten," and a boy just half-past four.

There is almost nothing, I think, that gives to children a greater sense of permanence, then to be *at home* in the natural world. Knowledge and understanding of the life that goes on around them out of doors gives them a respect for the pattern and order of the physical world; and pleasure in its beauty engenders a sense of proportion and tranquillity of spirit. In the autumn of 1940, when we were sore and sad for the hatefulness of what was going on in Britain, my daughter and I were unpacking the treasures from her room that had been put away for the summer. We came to her three Medici prints of Shakespeare's flowers, "Daisies pied and violets blue," "Lady-smock all silver-white," and "Fennel for you, and columbine and rue." She laid them out in a row, and looked at them for a long time. "Isn't it nice to think," she said, "that the same flowers that were blooming in Shakespeare's time are still coming up in Dorset? And no matter what happens now, they'll still be there when it's all over." Permanence, and beauty and peace; that was a comfortable thought.

One of our favorite stories in *Dobry* is Grandfather's account of the Creation: how God first made "very big, strong men—giants . . . to match up with the mountains, the trees, the four winds and great waters"; and how, when the giants were dissatisfied, he made a new kind of men, "dwarfs, very small, neatly made to match up with the grass blades, the fruit and the nutmeats." Then, because the dwarfs were not happy, "God peopled the earth anew with us middling-sized people, who can climb mountains, ride on the seas, and still know the clovers, hear the song of the robins and crickets. A middling-sized people who can love both perfection in bigness and perfection in littleness."

How good it is, to be middling-sized people!

CHAPTER TWELVE

Needle in a Haystack

O NE of the rather exhilarating things about maintain-
ing a house and family on a very limited budget, is
that of any two apparently necessary things, you can seldom
have both. You weigh and sift and balance the claims of
each demand, and having made your choice, you manage
somehow to go along happily without the thing you have
had to forego. We planned, early in our first child's school
career that we would invest in a good encyclopaedia, Comp-
ton's for preference. But every time we came within reach
of it, some more urgent need turned up, like a new baby,
or a motor for the boat that is our one means of reaching
the outside world in the summer.

So the matter has been allowed to rest. And as our daughter has progressed at school, and more and more things have
had to be looked up, we have found that there are ways of
finding information that are much more fun then just taking Vol. III: CRA–FRO, off the shelf and turning to the right
page. They are not quite so easy, of course, and a small
girl cannot manage quite so independently. But there is
value in that, too, for the whole family finds itself in hot

pursuit of some fact or material that gains in desirability as it eludes the pursuers. In the course of the search, you run across a great deal of information which, though it be quite irrelevant to the matter in hand, is both useful and interesting. It is like looking for the proverbial needle in the haystack, and learning, while you search, all sorts of practical and attractive facts about types of grasses, methods of constructing haystacks, the lore of husbandry, the appetites of farm stock and the delights of rural life.

For instance, quite lately our small student required material on Hawaii, the music or the volcanoes or the food. First of all we got out the big atlas and gathered a few notes, not very exciting, about volcanoes. Then there was a book somewhere about that had a chapter on Hawaiian food, but it proved to be by somebody who did not much care for food, and inclined to be heavily jocose about the Hawaiians' habits of eating; an attitude, we felt, not calculated to stimulate the interest nor broaden the view of a ten-year-old. One or two music books yielded a sparse crop of Hawaiian songs, with explanatory comments, and these we studied and reserved for use if nothing better turned up.

Then one of us suggested that *Harper's Magazine* was almost bound to have something useful, and we started through our ten years' volumes, knowing that even if the treatment of a topic should prove too erudite, we could help to sift out the pertinent information. Without going any farther back than 1938, we found one article on the volcanoes; one on the music; and one on the tabus that had a good deal to say about food. They were all authoritative, and all written with such lively enthusiasm that our young investigator found them palatable and provocative reading. They gave her precisely the kind of information she needed both for the immediate purpose of her school work, and for a general and intelligent knowledge of life in the Hawaiian Islands. The increment to the collaborators in research was high in proportion to the expense of effort: in addition to the very enlightening material on Hawaii, we found four splendid pre-war articles on affairs in the Pacific, that provided excellent background for our current newspaper reading; two beautiful short stories that we had forgotten about; and a poem that was poignantly beautiful and profoundly moving. I doubt that an equal amount of time spent with an encyclopaedia would have yielded half so much of real education.

Then there was the case of Mazeppa. He turned up in a volume of Currier and Ives prints that our child was examining with great interest. Her curiosity was aroused so that she wanted to know the whole story, but the text was so blurred in the reproduction that even a magnifying glass could not make it legible. Both father and mother were sure that, given time, they could remember what the pictures were all about. But it failed to emerge from the mists of memory, and our little inquirer was not content to wait indefinitely. So one afternoon after school she and I took the matter seriously in hand. First of all there was the dictionary appendix, "A Key to Noted Names in Mythology and Fiction," which we hoped would offer a clue. Finding none, we tried Bulfinch, thinking that perhaps the name

"Mazeppa" had remained in mind from reading myths and legends. We did not find what we were looking for, but we had lots of fun looking at the plates and talking about gods and goddesses.

Then suddenly I remembered Tchaikowsky's "Overture to Mazeppa"; I realized that I had never known precisely what it was the overture *to*, so we consulted Grove's Dictionary of Music and Musicians. "*Mazeppa,* an opera in three acts, by Peter Ilyitch Tchaikowsky, libretto from Pushkin's 'Poltava.' " We went through our one fat volume of Pushkin's *Tales* and "Poltava" was not there.

But this was the right moment to tell about "Papa" Pushkin; for a few evenings previously my husband and I had met and talked with a troupe of young Russian-Americans who gave a magnificent performance of Russian dances at a party given for the benefit of the Sulfa Drug Fund for the Soviet Army. We had been interested to know how they had learned to dance so superbly, and they told us about their homes, where dancing and story-telling were just as much a part of daily living as eating and sleeping. All of this we had told our daughter at breakfast the next morning, but what remained to be told now was that we had talked of Russian books: these young people almost tumbled over each other in their eagerness to ask if we knew this or that author, and one name bobbed about like a cork in the flood of conversation—Pushkin, Pushkin, Pushkin! So I told her what I knew about him, how he came to be known as the "people's poet," and how, as the young Russian dancers told us, every Russian child knows and loves him. This led into talk about the things that create unity in a nation; and about the defense of Stalingrad, which was then at its height, and a matter of vital, almost personal, concern to all of us. We talked of how people who are fighting for something they love and believe in, seem to be inspired by their conviction with more than human endurance and courage. We have had to be careful about discussing the war with our daughter because once or twice she had shown signs of painful emotional disturbance; but this time it came so naturally out of her interest in the people of Russia that I was able to clear up several points that were puzzling her, and incidentally to discover more than I ever had before about her attitude toward, and her understanding of, the war.

Presently we returned to our search; and all at once I remembered Byron's "Mazeppa." Out came the *Collected Poems of George Gordon, Lord Byron* and after I had answered, with help from the Biographical Notes, all her questions about who and what he was, we turned to the right poem. There was a prefatory "advertisement" in French from Voltaire. My collaborator said we could skip that, but I wanted to see if I could translate it, and she was just as much impressed by my ease and fluency as I was myself. We got out the French dictionary, to verify the exactness of one or two words in my translation and that was an opportunity to demonstrate the use of a foreign-language dictionary. Then we read the poem, and compared it with Voltaire's outline of the story and with what we could piece together of the text in the Currier and Ives engraving.

After two hours of perfectly delightful companionship, we arrived at the exact information we had set out to find and I venture to predict that neither one of us will forget it.

One of my treasured possessions is a stout black notebook in which for many years I have jotted down sentences and paragraphs and poems that have seemed to me for one reason or another to have importance. On one of the very first pages is a quotation from Aldous Huxley's *Antic Hay*, written large and boxed in with firm black lines: "Until all teachers are geniuses and enthusiasts, nobody will learn anything but what he teaches himself." The idea struck me with great force when first I met it. Now I think it is too limited: now I believe that even when teachers are geniuses and enthusiasts, what is most valuable in their work is their capacity for training people to teach themselves: to dig out information; to examine, select and relate facts; to draw conclusions, to preserve an open mind, and to gather up and salt away for future use, the incidental information that crops up along the edges of a line of search. Ideally this kind of teaching would be a big part of a parent's job, because the bent of the twig is determined long before he reaches his school years. He provides the stimulus toward such teaching by his own natural and persistent curiosity, and by his ability to comprehend and absorb all you give him in the way of satisfaction for that curiosity.

I suppose our present program of research with our daughter grew out of our habit of answering her questions as fully as we were able. Her "six honest serving-men" worked overtime, and the only way that we could see to

avoid madness was to cultivate a genuine interest in all the
things she wanted to know about, and to find out as much
about them as we could for our own benefit, as well as hers.
We were both surprised and pleased to find how much satisfaction and pleasure there was in taking her questions seriously and answering them honestly. We said, "You may ask
any reasonable question three times, and then don't you
think you should remember the answer?" The result was
that she tended less and less to ask questions aimlessly;
when she knew that she was going to get an answer that
was worth remembering, she concentrated her question
marks where they would do the most good. So she took the
first important step in her education by learning how to
ask questions.

Not very long ago she said to me with a twinkle, "Almost
the first thing I ever remember hearing you say was 'I don't
know, but I'll find out.' You're a terrible cautious person,
aren't you?" I laughed, because it seems only a week ago
that a pair of parents about two months old, solemnly
agreed that the "Mother and Father Know All" tradition
was too heavy a burden if you ever hoped to have any fun
with your children. "Let's show ours from the very beginning that we're not infallible!" We probably overdid it a
bit. One friend laughed at my caution in verifying a trifling
bit of information before I passed it on to my three-year-
old. "You are ignorant, aren't you, not knowing an ele-
mentary thing like that!" But the reward for us is that she
has just as great a respect for our capacity for learning as
we have for hers. We discovered quite a long time ago that

our library could provide reliable answers for most questions, but it has been interesting to find that it is still more than adequate to the demands of our daughter's expanding educational program. Like most family collections, its beginning was the combination of two units—the books assembled by each member of the partnership before marriage. It reflects the separate and joint interests of two people, over a period of years, and its great virtue comes from the fact that neither one of us was able to buy books carelessly, so those we did buy had the quality of unimpeachable authority and an enlightened point of view, as well as great literary merit. The same need for careful spending has governed the purchase of books for our joint collection, and while we have certainly spent many times the amount that a good encyclopaedia would have cost in the last twelve years, I think we have assembled a reference library much more interesting and authoritative, if narrower in subject matter, than any compilation would be.

An assembly of not more than two thousand books covers a broad field: history and biography, geography, travel and exploration, the arts (with an especially large and valuable section on music), archaeology, sociology, philosophy, religion, poetry, essays, drama and fiction. Good current magazines supply excellent material on the sciences, more up-to-date than an encyclopaedia would contain, and these also provide authoritative views of world affairs to supplement newspaper reports. We have no index for our library, but because our books are all alive, in the sense that they are in constant use, we are seldom at a loss for clues to the information we require. There are bookcases in every room in the house—even the kitchen has a shelf of cookbooks, ranging from strictly practical collections of recipes to one or two unusual works on the history and lore of cookery. Each bookcase contains one or two categories and the books are arranged alphabetically by author. The shelves are revised, library-fashion, as part of the routine of dusting, and the housekeeper can usually tell you exactly where to lay your hand on any book—"seventh from the left-hand end of the second shelf from the bottom in the bookcase in the upstairs hall"—proving that almost any sort of training can be turned to account in making a home.

We have a few standard reference books—a good dictionary, a good atlas, Bartlett's *Familiar Quotations,* several foreign-language dictionaries, a good edition of the *King James Bible* with a concordance; reliable bird, flower and tree guides; and some books essential to our particular interests, like Grove's *Dictionary of Music and Musicians,* Pratt's *New Encyclopaedia of Music,* and innumerable reference books on literature for children which are surprisingly useful in providing directions for finding information on all sorts of subjects.

Our daughter has acquired by imitation the habit of making use of a great variety of books. Her own library was quite naturally made up largely at first of fiction and poetry, but as her interests have turned definitely in certain directions we have provided reliable books to give authority to her study. For instance, ever since she was eight years old, the ballet has been a subject of fascinating interest

to her and we gave her Arnold Haskell's *Ballet,* as a good
"base" book to add understanding to her enjoyment of the
performances we took her to see. She has acquired several
other books of her own choice, and has made extensive use
of the public library, quite on her own initiative, to en-
large her knowledge of all phases of the art of the ballet.
This has been an entirely independent enterprise, and the
thoroughness of her research can be accounted for partly by
the fact that we have always had fun together finding out all
we could about the things we're interested in.

I think that if we had started off with cut and dried research in an encyclopaedia we should have missed much of
the excitement and pleasure we have had in tracking down
information in the books we live with, our familiar friends
that endear themselves to us by their revelations of unexpected usefulness and pointed interest. It is rather a mad-
cap method, this of picking up stray clues and following
them through a series of unrelated books. But it is a reliable
method; and it cultivates a sort of receptiveness and a quest-
ing habit of mind. It whets the curiosity and so sharpens the
appetite for learning that we become less and less satisfied
with information that comes from just one point of view.
It helps the memory to develop the habit of filing away
material with increased exactness, against the day when
some new problem of investigation will demand applica-
tion of a great miscellany of known facts.

It requires the efforts of the whole family and this is a
wonderful advantage, for it means that we share each other's
intellectual adventures. Father and mother can share ac-

cumulated knowledge and the fruits of a great range of reading with a mind that has a new way of learning, and an altogether fresh and stimulating point of view. Our small student takes us with her into all the pleasant places that her independent education is discovering for her, and we have all the fun of growing up with her, into new knowledge.

Even now, our four-year-old is beginning to respect information that comes out of books to illuminate his interests. His sister is his joyous companion in investigation; picture the two heads, one with sleek dark pigtails, and the other tousled and fair, bent over an atlas open at the map of India, looking for the spot where Black Sambo lived. We are already beginning to see what fun it will be when he joins in the search for knowledge among the crowded shelves of our spreading family bookcases. "A hunt in such a forest never wearies."

CHAPTER THIRTEEN

Some Funny Books

SOME books are funny to some people, other books are funny to other people; and people who find the same books funny can enjoy the interplay of reference, and the subtle sympathy of laughter that gives companionship a special intimacy. Our family has ten great favorites. It doesn't particularly matter *why* we find them amusing. The important thing is that we have the most wonderful fun reading them, talking about them, and quoting from them. They prick up points of light in all sorts of ordinary happenings, and, by association, add a peculiar piquancy to our enjoyment of people. Every one of them is known as a child's book, not so much because its appeal is limited to children, as because children can so heartily enjoy it. All of them are serviceable books, the kind you read and re-read, with a compound interest of pleasure, from the time you are a sprout till you share them—as we hope to do—with your grandchildren.

Winnie-the-Pooh was the first of our favorite funny books that we read to our daughter, and it had a sort of delayed action that made it seem even funnier. She took it all quite seriously at first, listening with wide-eyed enchantment to all the ridiculous, adorable adventures of Pooh and Piglet, Rabbit, Kanga, Eeyore and Owl, and never laughing at all. Then one evening when we two were sitting quietly with our books in the living-room, we heard sounds of muffled laughter from upstairs. Curiosity got the better of us after a while, and we went up to ask what the joke was. Our five-year-old was sitting up in bed, with crimson cheeks and dancing eyes, almost speechless with mirth because she had suddenly thought of Pooh, stuck in the doorway of Rabbit's house, with Christopher Robin at the north end of him, reading a Sustaining Book "to help and comfort a Wedged Bear in Great Tightness," and Rabbit hanging his washing on the south end.

After that, when we read *Winnie-the-Pooh* or the *House at Pooh Corner,* she laughed just as much as we did, and to this day we cannot get through some of the stories without dissolving into helpless laughter. We have almost forgotten that there is such a word as "elephant"; an elephant to us is a Horrible Heffalump, or a Herrible Hoffalump, or a Hellible Horralump or a Hoffable Hellerump. People move away uneasily when they meet us in zoos, because we go off into such gales of merriment and talk such a queer jargon. But we know what we mean. Anyone in our family who does a stupid thing is a Bear of No Brain at All; when our daughter went through a phase of patient resignation to being neglected and misunderstood, she was known as Eeyore. Nobody writes "Happy Birthday" any more—it is always "HIPPY PAPY BTHUTHDTH THUTHDA BTHUTHDY." An expedition is always an Expotition, between-meal refreshment is "a smackerel of something"; any sort of jollification is "Merriment, what ho!" *Winnie-the-Pooh* and *The House at Pooh Corner* are *infectious* books. I still resent the reviewer who dismissed them with "Tonstant Weader fwowed up." Any books that families can have such superior fun with are "the real thing."

Not very long ago my daughter and her father were sitting side by side on the couch, reading *The House at Pooh Corner*, one waiting for the other at the foot of each page, and both chuckling happily. When they came to the end of a chapter our daughter looked up with a grin. "Are you reading a children's book, or am I reading a grown-up book?" she asked. "Both," said her father emphatically.

Ferdinand is another sort of funny book, a mixture of drollery and burlesque that we find very palatable. The pictures are a delightful adjunct to the story, and part of the fun of quoting lies in the fact that words and phrases conjure up the appearance of things that amuse us. We particularly like the picture of Ferdinand sitting under his favorite cork tree. One of the reasons why we are especially enjoying *Ferdinand* just now is that Duff Secundus, who is still too little to share most of our funny books, is having *such* a good time with it. "Smelling the flowers just quietly" is a phrase that he might have made up himself, it is so like the things he says, and we three older ones bubble over every time he uses it. I hope he will say to me one day, as his sister did a year or two ago, "You are a very understanding mother, even though you are a cow."

One doesn't mind such reflections on one's appearance, knowing what they come from. My daughter has a very engaging custom of bringing me little tributes of flowers every now and again, always with a suitably inscribed card enclosed. Once when I had distinguished myself in some mild way, the card bore congratulations, handsomely engraved in silver, and below, in a somewhat wobbly hand, "With love from the Elephant's Child." I don't quite remember how long ago we began to read the *Just So Stories,* but it has been long enough for the language to become thoroughly assimilated into the family idiom. There is a richness of invention about these stories that almost takes your breath away; they are absurdly and hilariously funny, but we do not laugh very much when we read them for fear of missing something. But the flavor remains on the palate, and the words settle so securely into the memory that they keep the stories all alive for thinking about and enjoying afterwards. A favorite term of approval in our household is "man-of-infinite-resource-and-sagacity"; our children from the time they were fledglings have sent their food down into "the warm dark inside cupboards." A shirker is reproved with "Is it right to be so idle, with the world so new and all?" and we have only to call our daughter "Taffaimai Metallumai" if her manners require correction—she knows that it means "small-person-without-any-manners-who-ought-to-be-spanked." She used to talk at school about her " 'satiable curiosity," and when one of her companions asked her why she used such long words she stuck to her text and replied, "I always use long words. I'm a grown-up."

The *Just So Stories* are pleasantly associated with the life at our Georgian Bay cottage, because we regularly read them each summer. It is great fun to find how aptly many expressions fit into our conversation there. The woods behind the house we refer to as "the Altogether Uninhabited Interior." Our bay is "all set about with fever-trees," and the turtle who lives under the dock is called "Slow-and-Solid." Once, on a picnic, we cooked a rather peculiar stew over the fire, and when I asked our child how she liked it, she said "Nice—nice but nubbly." That same day when we were on the way home she said that my sunburned face "reflected the rays of the sun with more-than-oriental splendor."

Our funny little boy will be all ready for the *Just So Stories* when he is old enough to enjoy them, for the expressions are so familiar to him. When he occasionally refuses to come along with the rest of us on walks, his sister tells him that he is the "wild, wild cat, waving his tail and walking by his wild lone." If he disturbs her too much when she is busy with something, she threatens to "spank him with her hard, hard claw," for "dancing hornpipes when he shouldn't." What a wonderful book is this book that gives us so much fun when we read it, and goes with us everywhere ever after!

The Three Policemen is a book that lives more between its own covers than our other favorites. We do not quote from it nearly so much as from most, but we read it over and over again, enjoying the distinctive flavor of its nonsense. It is a very restful book; everything is so straightforward, uncomplicated and business-like. All the work goes through so expeditiously, and Young Botsford, our pet character, is so reliable and efficient. There is one passage that to us is exquisitely funny, the description of the three policemen being wakened punctually at seven-thirty, by a gramophone record, made by the mayor of Farbe Island.

It had a deep growling bass voice: it went something like this:
> Bong!—out of bed
> Bong!—wash, shave and brush your hair
> Bong!—put on your shirts and socks
> Bong!—trousers, belts and vests
> Bong!—on with boots and gloves
> Pling!—helmets and coats
> Good morning, gentlemen.

Young Botsford of Farbe Island was also wakened by a gramophone record which was set off by an alarm clock. His record was much shorter, however; it simply said: GET UP! GET UP! GET UP!

The Three Policemen was our daughter's introduction to mystery stories. If they were all as bland, as ingenious and as hilarious as this one, what fun they would be!

Mary Poppins and *The Wind in the Willows* are two books that fit into almost any category. Both have moments of real beauty; both have superb fairy-tale quality; both are full of the milk of human kindness, and both are funny, with a humor that is subtle and irresistible. The essential funniness of *The Wind in the Willows* is in the situations and the behavior of the characters; Mary Poppins is her own funniness. Pathos and sweetness are so mixed in with the drollery of the adventures of Ratty, Mole, Toad, and their friends that if you try to separate and analyze the element of laughter you lose the perfect balance of the whole; but Mary Poppins stands aloof from the situations she creates, and you can walk all around her and see why she is so unforgettably comical. We value these books because they both evoke much respect for human personality, and at the same time highlight its foibles and weaknesses with an indulgent humor. A vain person seldom seems wholly contemptible if you know Mary Poppins: a braggart seldom altogether vulgar when you remember that Toad was a little pathetic. We read these books because they are such glorious fun; but their lessons in understanding are as enduring as their laughter.

Our favorite funny families are the Poppers and the Peterkins. In *Mr. Popper's Penguins* you find a family who depart from all the conventional ways of family life and make it seem reasonable. They leave all the windows in the house open so that their penguins will be comfortably cold; they install a freezing plant in the basement (moving the furnace up to the living-room to make room for it) so that the penguins can raise a family, and when ten beautiful little penguins hatch out, the Poppers proceed to train them for a vaudeville act.

The troupe goes on tour, and everything happens! We laughed so hard when we first read about it that we had to stop reading to avoid hysterics. Now that we can control ourselves a little, we go over it slowly, dwelling on each episode, and savoring the utterly stupendous absurdity of it. The bit we all love the best is the first penguin's setting up housekeeping in the icebox. What he took in with him is the most extraordinary list of objects I know, and we can never read it without howls of laughter:

Two spools of thread, one white chess bishop, and six parts of a jigsaw puzzle. . . . A teaspoon and a closed box of safety matches . . . A radish, two pennies, a nickel, and a golf ball. Two pencil stubs, one bent playing card, and a small ash tray.

Five hairpins, an olive, two dominoes, and a sock . . . A nail file, four buttons of various sizes, a telephone slug, seven marbles, and a tiny doll's chair. . . .

Five checker pieces, a bit of graham cracker, a parchesi cup, and an eraser. . . . A door key, a buttonhook, and a crumpled piece of tinfoil. . . . Half of a very old lemon, the head of a china doll, Mr. Popper's pipe, and a ginger ale cap. . . . An inkbottle cork, two screws, and a belt buckle. . . .

Six beads from a child's necklace, five building blocks, a darning egg, a bone, a small harmonica, and a partly consumed lollipop. Two toothpaste lids and a small red notebook.

We love our friend Blair, who finds the list as funny as we do. She arrived at the door one Saturday morning almost hidden behind a tremendous armful of strangely assorted objects. "I've brought back some things of yours that we had," she said. "A flower-bowl and a package of cigarettes and two books and a bicycle pump and Deirdre's pajamas and some cookies and a pie plate—and half of a very old lemon!"

The Peterkins *would* be sane and orderly if they *could* be, but they have an inspired gift of dimwittedness. " 'If,' said Mrs. Peterkin, 'we could only be more wise as a family.' " It would be our loss if they were, for the remembrance of every ludicrous episode strike a chord in this family. No matter how badly we manage anything, nor however many mishaps occur, we can settle our nerves and calm our agitation by reflecting that we are no worse than the Peterkins, and things always turned out well for them. I am told that I play the alternating roles of Mrs. Peterkin and the Lady from Philadelphia, which is a comfortable balance; somebody has got to straighten things out, but it's rather fun to help to tangle them too.

Every single episode in the chronicles of the Peterkin family is the essence of pure "loopiness": Mrs. Peterkin's cup of coffee, the horse that wouldn't go; the piano that couldn't be played in cold weather; the Christmas tree that didn't fit; Elizabeth Eliza and her trunk; the mad Fourth of July celebration: the confusion that modern improvements created, and the Peterkins at the poorhouse—these are only the cream of the jest, and we read them over and over again, almost with awe of the brain that could devise such beautiful nonsense.

The Peterkins are wonderfully quotable. If there is a loud crash in the house, somebody is sure to say "Is anybody killed?" If we go off to a picnic place that someone has recommended, and find it quite impossible, we say "No strawberries and no nook, but there's a good place to tie the horses." If we oversleep in the morning, and have to scramble to get everybody off to school, we excuse ourselves with

"It is a very good thing to learn not to get up any earlier than is necessary."

Life would fall short of perfection without *The Peterkin Papers,* and still farther short without our other funny books. We wonder what could possibly be an adequate substitute for this partnership in merriment, in families who do not read together.

CHAPTER FOURTEEN

A Brief for Fairy Tales

MY favorite corner of the bookshop where I once pre-
sided over the children's books was the one where
the fairy tales lodged. For me, who as a child had never been
able to get enough of fairy tales, it was a wonderful thing to
live with all those volumes and volumes, potent with magic:
Grimm and Andersen, Joseph Jacob's *English Fairy Tales,*
Andrew Lang's "Color" fairy books, Winifred Hutchinson's tales of ancient Greece, wonder tales from all over the
world, *The Water Babies* and *Alice* and *The Three Mulla-
Mulgars,* and all the rest.

But selling them was another matter. The children who
came to buy were usually of the same mind as I was about
these things; but mostly it was grown-ups who came, seeking
gifts for young relatives or friends. And my suggestion of
fairy tales often met with a chilly response. "Oh, I don't
think modern children enjoy fairy tales"; or "Couldn't you
give me something interesting?" And once it was, "Indeed
no! I won't have my children reading such untruthful rubbish."

Now the term "fairy tale" as I use it does not necessarily

mean a story about fairies. It includes along with the literature of pixies, elves, leprechauns, and so on, all stories that
have the element of magic, of enchantment, of unseen forces
governing the course of events. It includes the folk tales that
were devised by our far-off ancestors, people without benefit of science and theology, to explain the source of life, the
nature of the universe, the vagaries of the elements and the
complexities of the human animal. It includes, further,
stories of imagination and fantasy written in modern times.
This is a very large segment of literature to dismiss with
"children don't enjoy it," or "it isn't interesting." As for its
being "untruthful rubbish," that is a little pathetic. The
mother who condemned fairy tales so forthrightly was a
thoughtful person anxious to do well by her children. But
she represented the elements that Anatole France described
as "looking upon the imagination with mistrust." If she
had herself been capable of exercising a little imagination,
she would have avoided the "facile error" of assuming that
because a thing is not literally true, beyond any shadow of
error, doubt, whimsy or suspicion, exactly according to
one's own knowledge and experience, it is wanting in any
element of truth, and is told only with intent to mislead
and possibly to corrupt.

Children do not as a rule make this mistake; they are not
so rigidly habituated to the distinctions that grown-ups
make between what is probable and possible and what is
inconceivable and contrary to reason. They still possess the
faculty of imagination that makes room for miracles, perhaps because the marvelous novelty of the world and of

living has not yet worn off. The trouble with grown-ups is that they take things too seriously. Where children read fairy tales—and they do read them—just for fun, grown-ups often tend to theorize about ethical, social and cultural values until all the juice is squeezed out.

Some years ago I spent a very stimulating afternoon lecturing to a group of parents about fairy tales, and why it is a good thing for children to read them. My remarks stirred up a regular hornet's nest. "What about all the killing that goes on? Do you think it's healthy for children to read about that?" "Isn't it a bad shock for a child's nervous system to read about people being boiled in oil?" "I remember reading fairy tales that condone behavior absolutely contrary to what I am trying to teach my children is right." "Don't you think children use fairy tales too much as a means of escape from their own environment and from responsibilities?" "Do you think it is a good thing for children to get the idea, as they do from fairy tales, that stepmothers are always cruel and unjust? I have a stepchild, and it makes me quite unhappy to find her reading such things." "Should children be told as much about tragedy and death as Andersen's fairy tales have in them?" "How are children to believe what they learn at Sunday School if so much that they read in fairy tales is the exact opposite?" "Don't you think it's confusing for children to hear about all the Greek gods, when we teach them that there is only one God?"

I know the answers to all those questions a great deal more surely now than I did then; for in the meantime I have lived with a little girl who "just adores" fairy tales.

But I answer them only for that one child; as I told my questioners, and as I still believe, "it all depends." Children differ so in sensitiveness, in perceptiveness, in experience, in environment, in intelligence, that it isn't sensible to expect one answer to any one question to settle the matter for all children.

It is not a particularly *healthy* thing for children to read about killing. Killing is not a healthy business. But it goes on just the same, and I think that reading about the matter-of-fact way that people have of disposing of their adversaries in fairy tales has perhaps helped to "condition" my daughter to withstand the shock of hearing and reading about the impassioned massacre that men indulge in nowadays. Children, after all, are a part of this world, and however little we and they like some aspects of it, it will not help to draw the veil over the unpleasant things. I know that with my own daughter there is no danger of developing a calloused point of view. Accepting a situation that you cannot do anything about for the moment is quite a different thing from absolving yourself of responsibility for the future, and it is possible that the knowledge that men from time immemorial have killed each other may be the basis of a practical method of discovering how to stop it. So if my gentle child *wants* to read about bloodthirsty doings, and shows no ill effects on nervous system or behavior, it is her own affair. She makes her own decisions about boilings-in-oil and other such robust episodes too. I have no doubt she skips any too graphic descriptions and this is her privilege.

The matter of "behavior patterns" in fairy tales is another thing that we take very casually, where our daughter is concerned. My impression is that people in fairy tales behave pretty much as people do in real life. Some live by high principles, some are given over to evil ways; some are kindly in disposition, others practice meanness and persecution. Some go adventuring, some stay at home. There are strong and weak people, honest and devious people, people with great intelligence, and many with little or none. And in fairy tales each type, with the action that represents it, is brought to life objectively, emphatically and consistently. Fairy tales do not "condone" behavior that is contrary to ethical principle. They simply recognize the fact that it occurs. The mother who was so flustered about the possible detriment to her children of reading fairy tales overlooked the fact that she herself had read them and still retained a well-developed sense of right and wrong. We have not observed any confusion of values or standards in our daughter's mind, as a result of reading fairy tales. She has once or twice remarked that some individual of her acquaintance reminded her of a specific character in a fairy tale, and it was so easy to see why, that we think she must have learned a good deal about the fundamental ways of human nature from her reading.

Then there is this business of "escape" from reality that bothered one of the mothers. I am beginning to be a little tired of that expression; it is nearly always used with a rather scornful accent, as if to escape were something a bit shameful, like tippling on the sly. People need to get away from the daily round, the common task every once in a

while; if they don't there is something wrong. And I do not
see why children should be any exception. Our daughter
"escapes" into all her books, and especially into fairy tales
because they conjure up a world so different from the work-
aday one; but I think they are no more likely than any
other form of diversion to seduce her from the path of duty.
If she ever did show a tendency to retreat too constantly into
books, I hope I should be acute enough to look for the cause
of her need to escape, rather than to quarrel with the means.
But I think such a situation is less likely to arise with a child
who is allowed to exercise her imagination and indulge her
taste for fantasy, through unrestricted freedom in the realm
of faërie.

There are occasions in this household, as in any other,
when parental authority has to be asserted with some vigor.
Once, when our daughter was a bit over three years old she
was being very difficult and slow about putting away her
toys. Finally her father lost patience, and in a proper drill-
sergeant's voice he bellowed, "Hurry up!" Without even
looking up, she remarked calmly, "Said the great big troll."
Another time, when I insisted that she do something she
wanted not to do, she said bitterly, "You're a cruel stepmother, that's what you are!"

I think this kind of thing indicates pretty clearly how
much the designation of a character in a fairy tale is likely
to influence a child's attitude toward a whole class. There
are one or two pretty formidable mothers in the tales our
daughter has read, but there is no reason why she should
invest me with their repellent characteristics for the sole

reason that I too am known as "mother." I quite see that a
stepmother might be a little sensitive about the stigma at-
tached to fairy-step-motherhood, but after all, the stepmother is a sort of stock figure, like the Hero, the Villain or
the Comic Character. And for two reasons, a child would be
unlikely to develop an unfriendly attitude toward her own
stepmother just from reading about the fairy-tale variety.
In the first place, the delineation of character in fairy tales
is so all-of-a-piece, and so forceful, that unless a living person showed the same intrinsic qualities as a person in a
story there would be no reason for confusing the two just
because they happen to have the same title. In the second
place, a child is more strongly influenced by personality
than by association of ideas; and most children have too
much common sense to let romantic ideas interfere with
their own personal relationships. I have heard several
people condemn the practice of reading fairy tales because
they are afraid that children will begin to be fanciful about
the people around them, but the only effect we have noticed
in our daughter is that she is more strongly aware of the
flavor of human personality.

Now we arrive at the question, whether children should
come up against tragedy and death, as they occur in Hans
Andersen's stories. My answer to that, based on our daughter's response to such things, is an emphatic "Yes!" For the
great beauty and enduring value of Hans Andersen's *Fairy
Tales* is that they show life as it is, birth at the beginning
and death at the end, and a whimsical mixture of laughter
and tears in between. I do not understand why it should be

thought right or necessary to shield a child from the knowledge that death is the inevitable, the logical, the adventurous end to living. I think he should know that none of us understands what comes afterwards, but that it is necessary to create, out of one's life, something worthy of survival. This idea must grow by slow and comfortable degrees, and I know of few things that show the way more simply and sweetly than Hans Andersen's stories. He does not twist things away from their natural direction in order to bring about a happy ending, and I think that children feel the dignity and tranquillity of his rounded episodes. Tragedy, in Andersen's tales, is never shocking; he is gentle and patient in teaching children that life does not always have a happy face, and his sense of proportion is so delicate that he never overburdens his readers with sadness. The persuasive feeling of quiet confidence and conviction of the rightness of things as they happen flows steadily through Hans Andersen's *Fairy Tales,* and I know it is helping our daughter to form her own philosophy of acceptance of the naturalness and inevitability of death and sorrow.

Whenever I hear objection made to fairy tales on the ground that they are in conflict with the teachings of the Christian faith, I think of the saying of Sri Ramakrishna: "As one can ascend to the top of a house by means of a ladder or a bamboo or a staircase or a rope, so divers are the ways and means to approach God, and every religion in the world shows one of these ways. Different creeds are but different paths to reach the Almighty.". . .

I think it is important for children to know that however

differently people in various times and places have explained the order of creation, and the nature of the Creator,
and the relationship of human beings to that Creator and
to each other, they were simply doing the best they could
to understand these things, and to govern their ways of life
and of worship by what they could learn from their experience of the world they lived in. The accounts and illustrations of their beliefs and customs that come down to us in
folk tales are a child's first introduction to comparative religion. He will have a better understanding of our beliefs
and principles if he knows something of how they evolved,
and he is not likely to have less respect for what he is taught
at home and at church because of knowing. In our daughter's case, the reading of folk and fairy tales has given a
broader, richer and sweeter conception of Omnipotence
than she ever would have had if we had held her to familiarity only with the stories of the Christian faith. Fairy tales
have taught her that "there be divers things both natural
and supernatural that Man with his intelligence cannot
seize upon nor explain," and her attitude toward the universe and the force and authority that regulate it, is a blend
of curiosity, open-mindedness and genuine wonderment.

When she was two years old, something happened that
seemed rather marvelous to us, and apparently quite normal to her. We were staying in a little "villa" on the out-
skirts of a West-coast Scottish town, and every morning
before breakfast we went for a walk, up the road, under a
bridge, and past a meadow where there was a little copse beside a tiny waterfall. The first time we went, she stopped by

the meadow and called "Hello, boy." We saw no boy, but were used enough to her fanciful ways to suppose that she had imagined somebody there. The second morning she did it again, smiling and waving her hand as to a friend. The next day it was raining, and we thought of staying indoors, but she said, "The boy is waiting. I want to see him," and persuaded us into mackintoshes for our usual stroll. She would tell us nothing about her friend, apparently assuming that we were bright enough to see for ourselves what he was like. Then three years later, when we were in Scotland again, she suddenly asked one day, "Who was the boy I saw by the wee burnie?" We said we didn't know, and asked her what he looked like. "He had a brown overall on," she said, "and a bright green pointed cap." Now nobody had ever told her how elves and leprechauns look; this was something that she had seen for herself. Maybe it was only a chance effect of tree trunk and leaves, but for her it *was* a little man in a green cap, playing his own games among the green grass and the heather. Wiser people than she have seen fairies before now.

So it was not surprising to us that when she began to read, fairy tales formed a substantial part of her diet. We were glad because we remembered how we had loved them, and it was delightful to see what wonderful fun she was having. Last summer, when she had finished reading for the third or fourth time Eleanor Farjeon's *Martin Pippin in the Daisy Field*, she said, "I hope I'll never be too old to read fairy tales." She probably never will, for what she has got in pleasure and learning from her excursions into all forms and variations of fairy tales constitutes a resource that age cannot wither. She, like the Brothers Grimm, has "sought to penetrate the wild forests of our ancestors, listening to their noble language, watching their pure customs, recognizing their ancient freedom and hearty faith."

She is at home in fairyland, and she knows now and will continue to know, that "its sweet playfulness and merry serviceableness and wintry, patient sadness are all one with the common world that shines for everybody."

CHAPTER FIFTEEN

Letter to a Grandfather

Twelfth Night, 1943.

DEAR D. D.:

This is the last day of Christmas. This afternoon we dismantled our tree and set it out in the garden, sprinkled with grain and hung with pieces of suet for the birds. Tonight we burned our greens, the mistletoe from the hall, the "wesselbob" from the front door, and all the sprays and garlands that made the living-room so festive. Now the children are tucked into bed, the fire has settled to a quiet glow, and the house has its everyday look again.

It has been a beautiful Christmas. We began our festivities, as we always do, on St. Nicholas Eve, with the wrapping of gifts for our Canadian families. It seemed strange, not to be doing yours too; posting them in October seems rather unfestive, somehow. But we thought about you, and hoped that you would have a happier Christmas than the last three have been. We sang every day, all the carols and songs we knew, and learned many that we had never sung before, lovely ones from France and Holland, Czechoslovakia, Poland and the other countries where people wouldn't

have the heart for singing. And every evening, as we worked
at our gift-making, we listened to records. Even the little lad
had his favorite music, and listened with great contentment,
while he had his rest after lunch, to all the lovely tranquil
things like *The Shepherd's Christmas Music,* the Corelli
Christmas Concerto, and that beautiful little Sciassi *Christmas Symphony* that we told you about when first we discovered it.

I had a particularly happy time, helping with the program of tableaux that are part of the celebrations at school
each year. When I was asked to suggest something a little
different from the masterpieces of the Nativity that have
always been used, I was very pleased. For I had been thinking that we should remember in some concrete fashion the
children of Europe who have lost their Christmas. We called
the performance "Light the Candles"; the stage was set with
a little house, the kind you see in pictures of German fairy-
tales, with snow hanging from the eaves and little fir-trees
flanking the wide window in which the pictures were
shown. Five tremendous candles stood in a row at one side.
We printed Ruth Sawyer's lovely poem from *The Long
Christmas* at the top of the program, so that people could
read it and get the feeling of what we intended:

> Send forth the star;
> And, Mary, take his hand—
> He may not understand
> How changed we are.
> Light towering candles; rim
> The earth with them.

Let angels sing "Amen"
To His birth-hymn.
Let thy sweet laughter
When he was born
Fill this dark morn—
Sky rafter to rafter.

Mary, thou canst see
Between the suns
The road that runs
From manger to Calvary.
Let him not feel our dole
Of hate and gall;
He is too small
For agony of soul.
Make then his coming bright
On earth; let every door
Swing wide with peace; nor
Let one evil thing blot out the night.

When the house lights went down, and before the stage was
lit, one of the students read a preamble that went like this:
"For the past ten years and more, the Christmas candles
have been going out one by one, all over Europe. First of all
in Germany, where for generations the *Krist-Kind* had
found a loving welcome in happy homes, the Christmas
lights flickered and grew dim, and the darkness came. Because of that darkness, every country in Europe has lost its
festive lights—Austria and Czechoslovakia, Poland and the
Lowlands, Italy and Spain, the Scandinavian countries, and
all the little countries of Middle Europe.

"We believe that one day the candle flames will shine again. And since Christmas is always and everywhere a festival for children, we are going to light a handful of candles today with pictures showing the ways in which Christmas was celebrated by the children of Europe in the old happy days.

"It is not possible to light a candle for every country, but the five symbolic lights that we shall kindle here represent our faith and hope that the Christ Child will come once more, in gentleness and peace, to Europe and to all the world; and that the light will shine again on high-hearted Christmas revels."

Then the first tableau came into brightness in the little house: "The Toy Making," suggested by a picture in Hill and Maxwell's *Rudi of the Tollgate,* and the whole school sang "Silent Night" in German. As the curtains closed over the scene, the first candle flame was lit. There was a picture from Libushka Bartusek's *Happy Times in Czechoslovakia,* with the A Cappella Choir singing the Czech Carol "Strangers Say a King is Born"; Poland was represented by a tableau based on Stryjenska's painting, *Christmas,* and the Choir sang the Polish "Lullaby Carol." Jan Steen's *The Eve of St. Nicholas* made a beautiful picture for the Lowlands, and the music was especially lovely too, Di Lasso's *"Adoramus Te, Christe,"* pure and sweet in those fresh young voices. The last tableau, for the children of France, was Geraerd David's *Rest on the Flight into Egypt,* with "The Carol of the Birds" sung by the A Cappella Choir. As each tableau ended, another candle was lit, and at the end, when all five of them were shining against the dark curtains, the Christmas Choir (about fifty voices, both boys and girls) burst out singing "Break forth, O beauteous heavenly light." It was all very beautiful and very moving, and I think that both the children who did the tableaux and the students and parents who saw them had a real understanding of what we had tried to do.

This school affair was very much a part of our family Christmas, for we discussed it together, D. lent her books for suggestions, R. and I planned the music and he trained the various groups who sang it.

D. wanted to make a very special gift for a teacher who has been a good friend to all of us, and the tableaux gave her an idea. She got a friend to help her, a little Scots girl from Aberdeen, and together they planned a series of tableaux to do for Miss Griffin. They asked for no help at all, but chose the pictures they would do, planned the costumes, gathered up the properties and decided what records they would play, all by themselves. I arranged a little stage for them, in the arch between the living-room and the sunroom, a folding screen draped with cream-colored monkscloth for the background, a little spruce tree for "atmosphere," and a curtain to draw over the scenes. D. invited her guests for one afternoon just before Christmas, and when we had had tea, the two little girls gave their performance. First they did Fra Angelico's *The Annunciation*, while the gramophone played Arcadelt's "Ave Maria."

Then came Fra Lippo Lippi's *Virgin Adoring the Child,*
with "And the Glory of the Lord," from the *Messiah* as
musical accompaniment; and finally David's *Rest on the
Flight into Egypt* with Jean Planel singing "The Holy
Family Resting by the Wayside," from Berlioz' *L'enfance
du Christ.*

It was extraordinarily beautiful; there was a simplicity
and sweetness about it that I found very affecting. The gift
was received as lovingly as it was given, and it was delightful to see such happiness.

We had the usual pleasant hurry and confusion about
getting all our presents ready, but we managed everything
by Christmas Eve, and had time to enjoy decorating the tree
and setting out all the ornaments that we keep from Christmas: the little white German Madonna, who stands in a
bower of greenery on the piano; the Jubilee procession with
the State Coach, the Household Guards, the Yeomen and
Dragoons, that march along the top of a bookcase, led by
the band of the Grenadier Guards; on the mantle, my little
crèche with the tiny figures that R. carved out of cedar wood
for our first Christmas; and the German villages and farms
that make such a charming decoration on our table.

Our ceremonies for Christmas morning you know about.
We followed our usual order of procedure, opening our
stockings in bed, before the festive breakfast with Kirstie's
red and white linen to make the table gay. But before we
went in to the tree, we did something special because of our
feeling that this Christmas should be thoughtful as well as
merry. We made a little ceremony of kindling the living-

room fire; all of us sat on the floor while R. set it alight, and
I read the ancient Celtic rune, "The Blessing of the Kindling":

I will kindle my fire this morning
In presence of the holy angels of heaven,
In presence of Ariel of the loveliest forms,
In presence of Uriel of the myriad charms,
Without malice, without jealousy, without envy,
Without fear, without terror of anyone under the sun,
But the Holy Son of God to shield me.
  Without malice, without jealousy, without envy,
  Without fear, without terror of anyone under the sun,
  But the Holy Son of God to shield me.

God, kindle thou in my heart within
A flame of love to my neighbor,
To my foe, to my friend, to my kindred all,
To the brave, to the knave, to the thrall,
O Son of the loveliest Mary,
From the lowliest thing that liveth,
To the Name that is highest of all.
  O Son of the loveliest Mary,
  From the lowliest thing that liveth,
  To the name that is highest of all.

In spite of their impatience to see the tree, the children
were very sweet and solemn. D., I think, understood our reason for pausing in the midst of the merry-making, and she
loved the words of the rune. S. will listen to almost anything
that is read to him, so he was happy too, and he knew with-

out being told that there was something important to us in
what we were doing. After that, the Day was all gaiety and
"sweet content," with much music and hearty laughter, and
a general feeling of happiness.

Our holiday was uneventful but satisfying. We went
once with D. to the Ballet Russe, and she was taken a second time by some friends who take great pleasure in watching her delight in every detail of it. Students came to tea
almost every day, which is always great fun, and several
evenings we spent with friends, just sitting around the fire
talking, very companionable and pleasant. Our Christmas
tree had yielded a fine crop of books, *The Tree of Life* for
me, and de la Mare's *Come Hither,* which I have badly
wanted ever since I lost my first copy; Specht's *Life of
Brahms* for R. and nearly a dozen fine books for each of the
children. So we read a great deal, and talked about what
we were reading, and learned much about each other. We
had lots of music, too. We were extravagant in buying records for each other because there are lean years coming and
we shall need our "hyacinths." There are few ways that I'd
rather spend an evening than listening to a program of our
own choosing, played and sung by the finest musicians in
the world. Isn't it a wonderful thing, to be able to have such
pleasures at home? Both of the children are good listeners,
and even the little 'un has a nice taste in choosing his own
records. He amazes us by his rapidity in identifying music
that he has heard before, and liked, and his delight in his
newly established record collection is beautiful to behold.

We always make a great occasion of Twelfth Night, for

we are reluctant to let Christmas slip away, and this time we lingered over each little ritual, to make the end of this especially beautiful Christmas quite perfect. We brought the greens and laid them on the hearth after supper, and lit all the Christmas candles and the bayberry dip that D. made us three years ago, which we always keep just for Twelfth Night. Then we sang our carols for the last time before putting them away for another year.

We gathered around the fire while I read "The Feast of Fools," the last of the stories in *The Long Christmas* which we read, one each evening, for the Twelve Days. Then we each in turn dropped a sheaf of green onto the fire, making a secret wish while it burned. S. didn't keep his secret, of course, but we knew anyway that it would be—"anither train with a green caboose." When our wishes have all gone up the chimney, we make prophecies of what good things each month of the New Year will bring, and it is pleasant to find that we all value the same things. Then we read Eleanor Farjeon's "A Round for the New Year" and "A Wish." Do look these up and read them; "A Wish" is particularly pertinent to these times. D. read the Herrick "Ceremonies for Candlemas" this year, and they seemed nicer than they ever have before.

A great deal of good talk and laughter was mixed in with all these doings, and it was lovely fun to have S. taking part and enjoying it for the first time; D's delight in all he does and says is perfectly charming. He was pretty sleepy by the time we brought in the spiced cider and shortbread, so he drowsed contentedly in R.'s arms while we ate and drank,

and put an end to our Christmas by reading Hans Andersen's "Twelve by the Mail." He was asleep almost before
we got him into bed, but D. lingered about downstairs, not
wanting, as she said, "to say good-by to the loveliest Christmas we've ever had."

After she had gone up, the two of us sat talking for a long
time. You see, this has been the first year when the war has
had any impact at all on our children's lives, and while as
yet it isn't very great, we were interested to discuss whether
it was upsetting D.'s standards at all. S. is too little yet to
know what is going on, but we want to be sure that when he
is older, and subject to the influence of upheaval, he will
have "spiritual bulwarks" to keep him safe.

Looking back over the year, we are reassured to find that
all the things that have had the greatest importance to us
and to the children are on the credit side of the ledger. We
have been happy in ourselves and with each other, and we
still believe in all the things that have always seemed to us
most worth having. Economically, life is a bit hazardous,
but I think we shall manage a necessary minimum of crea-
ture comforts, and we are not apprehensive for the future.
For the greatest pleasures and satisfactions that we and our
bairns have had this year have been what we call "the good
old imponderables": just being together, and laughing,
and reading books and hearing and making music; enjoying
the loveliness of out-of-doors, and the spaciousness of our
days in Georgian Bay; loving our friends and sharing their
view of life; thinking and speculating and exploring our
own minds and each others. But mostly just being together!

D. is not unaware of the seriousness and tragedy of the war. A few days before Christmas I was working in the kitchen, with a news summary coming over the radio in the living-room. The reporter read the newly released account of Nazi losses at Stalingrad, deaths mounting into astronomical figures. D. came to me with tears streaming down her face. "Oh, Mummy, think of all those German children whose fathers will never come home." I was overwhelmed with compassion for her vulnerable heart, and filled with thankfulness that she can see the pitifulness of human grief in a war that is so much too big for her to understand. But she has a sense of proportion, too, and respect for the toughness and persistence of the human race. She and our little man live with things that have beauty and permanence. Don't worry about your grandchildren. They'll be all right.

Yours aye,

A. D.

Appendix

Appendix

These lists contain recommended books and phonograph records, and sources for obtaining prints for a family art collection.

CHAPTER I

Becker, May Lamberton *First Adventures in Reading: Introducing Children to Books.* Stokes.

Dalgliesh, Alice. *First Experiences with Literature.* Scribner.

De la Mare, Walter. *Early One Morning in Spring; Chapters on children and on childhood as it is revealed in particular in early memories and in early writings.* Macmillan.

Eaton, Anne T. *Reading with Children.* Viking Press

Mahony, Bertha E. and Whitney, Eleanor. *Realms of Gold in Children's Books.* Doubleday, Doran.

—— *Five Years of Children's Books: A Supplement to Realms of Gold.* Doubleday, Doran

Moore, Anne Carroll. *My Roads to Childhood: Views and Reviews of Children's Books.* Doubleday, Doran.

Richards, Laura E. *What Shall the Children Read?* Appleton-Century.

CHAPTER II

Brooke, Leslie. *Johnny Crow's Garden.* Warne.

—— *Johnny Crow's Party.* Warne.

Brooke, Leslie. *Ring o' Roses*. Warne.

Caldecott, Randolph. *Picture Books*. (16 volumes). Warne.

Castor, Père. *Allons vite.*[1] Flammarion.

———— *My Book of Animals* [1] Flammarion.

Chansons de France pour les petits français.[1] Plon.

Crane, Walter. *The Baby's Bouquet*. Warne.

———— *The Baby's Opera*. Warne.

Eisgruber, Elsa. *Spin, Top, Spin*. (now out of print) Macmillan.

Gág, Wanda. *The A.B.C. Bunny*. Coward-McCann.

Greenaway, Kate. *Mother Goose*. Warne.

———— *Humpty Dumpty and Some Funny People*. Macmillan.

Lathrop, Dorothy. *Who Goes There?* Macmillan.

Le Mair, Willebeek. *Little Songs of Long Ago*. McKay.

———— *Our Old Nursery Rhymes*. McKay.

Petersham, Maud and Miska. *The Christ Child*. Doubleday, Doran.

Peterson, C. O. *Puti-puts Abenteuer.*[1] Scholz of Mainz.

Three Little Kittens. Macmillan.

Tuwim. *Locomotive*. Il. by Lewitt and Him. Minerva. (Imported)

———— *Vieilles chansons et rondes pour les petits français.*[1] Plon.

CHAPTER III

Bannerman, Helen. *Little Black Sambo*. Stokes.

———— *Sambo and the Twins*. Stokes.

Burton, Virginia Lee *Choo-Choo, the Story of a Little Engine Who Ran Away*. Houghton Mifflin.

———— *The Little House*. Houghton Mifflin.

Donaldson, Lois. *Smoky, the Lively Locomotive*. Whitman.

Gramatky, Hardie. *Little Toot*. Putnam.

Hurd, Clement. *The Race*. Random House

Lenski, Lois. *The Little Aeroplane*. Oxford University Press.

———— *The Little Auto*. Oxford University Press.

———— *The Little Farm*. Oxford University Press.

[1] Although these are imported, some of the large bookshops that make a specialty of foreign books may still have copies available.

Lenski, Lois. *The Little Sail Boat* Oxford University Press.
———— *The Little Train.* Oxford University Press.
Our Trains. Dean. (Imported)
Piper, Wally *The Little Engine That Could.* (Retold from *The Pony Engine.* Mabel C. Bragg) Platt & Munk.
Potter, Beatrix. *The Tale of Peter Rabbit.* Warne.
———— *The Tale of Tom Kitten.* Warne.
Rey, H. A. *How Do You Get There?* Houghton Mifflin.
Trains. Nelson. (Imported)

CHAPTER V

Barker, Cicely Mary. *Old Rhymes for All Times.* Blackie.
An unusual and delightful collection of traditional rhymes, beautifully illustrated.
Brooke, L Leslie. *Ring o' Roses.* Warne.
A small collection, but perfect in every respect for nursery use.
Harrington, Mildred P., compiler. *Ring-a-Round.* Macmillan.
An attractive collection made for three children "rising six," and approved by them. Pleasant black and white pictures by Corydon Bell.
Huffard G. T. and Carlisle, L. M., compilers. *My Poetry Book.* Winston.
A wide and varied anthology of modern poetry, covering a wide range of age appeal.
The Real Mother Goose. Rand McNally.
A very full collection for parents, and not unattractive for a child's use, though physically too large.
Thacher, L. W. S. and Wilkinson, M. O., compilers. *The Listening Child.* Macmillan. (Children's Classics)
This generous collection, for children of all ages, contains much that is pleasant to use with little ones A good source book.
Thompson, Blanche Jennings, compiler. *Silver Pennies.* Macmillan.
A good small collection of verses, nicely decorated. Most children seem not to be bothered by the rather stilted introductions to the poems.

Untermeyer, Louis, compiler. *This Singing World*. Harcourt, Brace.
A fine stimulating collection, with particularly good nonsense.

CHAPTER VI

Bullett, Gerald. *The English Galaxy of Shorter Poems*. Macmillan.
De la Mare, Walter. *Come Hither*. Knopf.
Drinkwater, John. *The Way of Poetry*. Houghton Mifflin.
Pocock, Guy. *A Poetry Book for Boys and Girls*. Dutton.
Repplier, Agnes. *A Book of Famous Verses*. Houghton Mifflin.
Thomas, Edward. *Poems and Songs for the Open Air*. Cape.
(This may not be readily available, but is included because it is so especially good.)
Untermeyer, Louis. *This Singing World*. Harcourt, Brace.
Wilkinson, Marguerite. *New Voices*. Macmillan.

CHAPTER VII

Fowler, H. W. and F. G. *The King's English*. Oxford University Press.
Fowler, H. W. *A Dictionary of Modern English Usage*. Oxford University Press.
Herbert, A. P. *What a Word!* Doubleday, Doran.
Mencken, H. L. *The American Language: An Enquiry into the Development of English in the United States* Knopf.
Roget, Peter. *Thesaurus of English Words and Phrases*. (Revised by Andrew Boyle and Charles Lee) 2 vols. Dutton.
Smith, Logan Pearsall. *Words and Idioms*. Houghton Mifflin.
Trench, Richard Chenevix. *The Study of Words and English, Past and Present*. Dutton.

CHAPTER VIII

Berry, Ana M. *Art for Children*. Boni.
Craven, Thomas. *A Treasury of Art Masterpieces*. Simon & Schuster.
Gibson, Katherine. *Pictures to Grow Up With*. Studio Publications.
Roas, Frank J. *An Illustrated Handbook of Art History*. Macmillan.

SUGGESTIONS FOR A FAMILY ART COLLECTION

NOTE: We have collected our prints over a period of years from so many different sources that no definite directions can be given. But the suggestions made here will be found reliable by any family that wishes to establish an "art collection" of its own. It is advisable, wherever possible, to compare the colors of a print with the original or with a good large reproduction. A photograph of a painting is better than a print in which the colors are poor and out of balance.

Most art galleries have good prints of their own pictures, available at not too great a cost for the smaller sizes. Lists are usually available, with prices stated.

The Medici Prints are available from Hale, Cushman and Flint, 857 Boylston Street, Boston, Massachusetts.

The Museum of Fine Arts, Boston, Massachusetts, issues portfolios giving "a survey of cultural history through reproductions of selected works of art with text." A list is available upon request.

The New York Graphic Society, 10 West 33rd Street, New York, has a fine list of reproductions. An illustrated catalogue is available, at a small cost.

The Phaidon Press, 114 Fifth Avenue, New York, issues a fine series of books on individual painters, with good colored illustrations. List upon request.

The Studio, a British art magazine, is still available at some bookshops, and contains color plates worth saving *The Studio Annual* of almost any year has large numbers of very attractive colored reproductions of paintings by various masters.

The Hyperion Press of New York Inc. % Duenewald Printing Corp., 218 West 18th Street, New York, publishes a series of monographs with colored illustrations on such artists as Degas and Goya.

CHAPTER IX

LIST OF RECORDS MENTIONED

The Children's Overture: Roger Quilter—London Philharmonic Orchestra (Barbirolli)—Victor 36370.

Christmas Concerto: Corelli—Members of State Opera Orchestra, Berlin (Weissmann)—Columbia, 2 twelve-inch records, Nos. 68075, 68076.

Excerpts from Hansel and Gretel: Humperdinck—Die Duoptisten and the Berlin State Opera Orchestra (Clemens Schmalstich)— Victor, 3 ten-inch records, Nos. 25168, 25169, 25170, Container J-7.

The Holy Family Resting by the Wayside: Berlioz—Orchestre Symphonique de Paris (Ruhlmann; Jean Planel, tenor)— Columbia P-69340-D.

The Moldau: Smetana—Czech Philharmonic Orchestra (Rafael Kubelik)—Victor Album M-523 (3 twelve-inch records).

Peter and the Wolf: Prokofieff—Boston Symphony Orchestra (Koussevitsky)—Victor Album M-566 (3 twelve-inch records).

Shakespearean Songs (arr. Walter)—Leslie French (tenor) with instrumental accompaniment. 4 sides, 2 twelve-inch imported discs —Gramophone Shop.

Shepherds' Christmas Music (from "The Christmas Oratorio"): J. S. Bach—Philadelphia Symphony Orchestra (Stokowski)— Victor 7142.

Songs from Shakespeare's Plays—Sung by Marie Houston (soprano) with Frank La Forge (harpsichord and piano) and Julius Gelfius (flute)—Victor (6 ten-inch records) Album V-P39.

Sweet Honey-Sucking Bees: Wilbye (with Ah, Dear Heart)—London Madrigal Group—Victor 4317.

Till Eulenspiegels Lustige Streiche. Richard Strauss—B. B. C. Symphony Orchestra (Fritz Busch)—Victor, 2 twelve-inch records, Nos. 11724–11725.

Tunes from The Baby's Opera—Alexander Schmidt, violin, and Myrtle Eaver, piano—Victor 24530.

Winnie-the-Pooh and *Christopher Robin:* Fraser-Simpson—Frank Luther, tenor—Decca 1389–1390.

CHAPTER X

Angelo, Valenti. *The Hill of Little Miracles.* Viking Press.
Bannerman, Helen. *Little Black Sambo.* Stokes.

Bartushek, Lubushka. *Happy Times in Czechoslovakia.* Knopf.

Bazin, René. *Juniper Farm.* Macmillan.

Bose, Irene Mott. *Totaram.* Macmillan.

Buff, Mary and Conrad. *Kobi, a Boy of Switzerland.* Viking Press.

Camp, Helen Orton. *The Story of Markets.* Harper & Brothers.

Clarke, Margery. *The Poppy Seed Cakes.* Doubleday, Doran.

Coatsworth, Elizabeth. *Away Goes Sally.* Macmillan.

Eberle, Ermingarde. *Spice on the Wind.* Holiday House.

Fischer, Marjorie. *Street Fair.* Smith & Haas.

Garnett, Eve. *The Family from One End Street.* Vanguard Press.

Govan, Christine Noble. *Those Plummer Children.* Houghton Mifflin.

Justus, May. *Peter Pocket's Luck.* Doubleday, Doran.

Lattimore, Eleanor Frances *Little Pear.* Harcourt, Brace.

Malot, Hector. *Nobody's Girl.* Cupples & Leon.

Mazer, Sonia. *Masha, a Little Russian Girl.* Doubleday, Doran.

Means, Florence Crandall. *A Candle in the Mist.* Houghton Mifflin.

Nesbit, E. *The Bastable Children.* Coward-McCann.

Petersham, Maud and Miska. *The Story Book of Food.* Winston.

Potter, Beatrix. *The Tale of Jeremy Fisher.* Warne.

———— *The Pie and the Patty Pan.* Warne.

Ransome, Arthur. *The Coot Club.* Lippincott.

———— *Swallowdale.* Lippincott.

———— *Swallows and Amazons.* Lippincott.

———— *We Didn't Mean to Go to Sea.* Macmillan.

———— *Winter Holiday.* Lippincott.

Rowe, Dorothy. *The Moon's Birthday.* Macmillan.

Sawyer, Ruth. *Roller Skates.* Viking Press.

Sayers, Frances Clarke. *Tag-Along Tooloo.* Viking Press.

Shannon, Monica. *Dobry.* Viking Press.

Simon, Charlie May. *Bright Morning.* Dutton.

Singer, Caroline, and Baldridge, LeRoy. *Boomba Lives in Africa.* Holiday House.

Smalley, Janet. *Rice to Rice Pudding.* Morrow.

Wilder, Laura Ingalls. *Little Town on the Prairie.* Harper & Brothers.

Wilder, Laura Ingalls. *The Long Winter*. Harper & Brothers.
———— *On the Banks of Plum Creek*. Harper & Brothers.
———— *On the Shores of Silver Lake*. Harper & Brothers.

CHAPTER XI

Barbellion, W. N. P. *The Journal of a Disappointed Man*. Double-day, Doran.
Burton, Virginia Lee. *The Little House*. Houghton Mifflin.
Comstock, H. J. *Insect Life: An Introduction to Nature Study*. Appleton-Century.
Curtis, Carlton. *A Guide to the Trees*. Greenberg.
Dunham, Elizabeth Marie. *How to Know the Mosses*. Houghton Mifflin.
Durand, Herbert. *A Field Book of Common Ferns*. Putnam.
Gissing, George. *The Private Papers of Henry Ryecroft*. Dutton.
Grahame, Kenneth. *The Wind in the Willows*. Scribner.
Holland, W. J. *The Butterfly Book*. Doubleday, Doran.
Housman, A. E. *A Shropshire Lad*. Holt.
Mills, Enos. *The Romance of Geology*. Doubleday, Doran.
Olcott, William Tyler. *A Field Book of the Stars*. Putnam.
Potter, Beatrix. *The Fairy Caravan*. McKay.
———— *The Tale of Mr. Tod*. Warne.
Reed, Chester. *The Flower Guide*. Doubleday, Doran.
———— *Land Birds East of the Rockies*. Doubleday, Doran.
———— *Water Birds East of the Rockies*. Doubleday, Doran.
Salten, Felix. *Bambi*. Simon & Schuster.

CHAPTER XIII

Atwater, Richard and Florence. *Mr. Popper's Penguins*. Little, Brown.
Du Bois, William Pène. *The Three Policemen*. Viking Press.
Hale, Lucretia P. *The Peterkin Papers*. Houghton Mifflin.
Kipling, Rudyard. *The Just So Stories*. Macmillan.
Leaf, Munro. *Ferdinand*. Illustrated by Robert Lawson. Viking Press.

Milne, A. A. *The House at Pooh Corner*. Dutton.

—— *Winnie-the-Pooh*. Dutton.

Travers, P. L. *Mary Poppins*. Reynal & Hitchcock.

—— *Mary Poppins Comes Back*. Reynal & Hitchcock.

CHAPTER XIV

Andersen, Hans. *Stories and Tales*. Houghton Mifflin.

Armfield, Constance. *The Wonder Book of the World*. Harcourt, Brace.

Asbjornsen, Peter Christian. *East of the Sun and West of the Moon*. Doubleday, Doran.

Aulnoy, Marie Catherine, Comtesse de. *D'Aulnoy's Fairy Tales*. McKay.

Barrie, J. M *Peter and Wendy* Scribner.

—— *Peter Pan in Kensington Gardens*. Scribner.

Carroll, Lewis. *Alice's Adventures in Wonderland*. Macmillan.

—— *Through the Looking Glass*. Macmillan.

Cendrars, Blaise. *The Epic of Kings: Hero Tales of Ancient Persia*. McKay.

—— *Little Black Stories for Little White People*. Putnam.

Colum, Padraic. *The Adventures of Odysseus and the Tale of Troy of the Children's Homer*. Macmillan.

—— *The Big Tree of Bunlahy*. Macmillan.

—— *The Island of the Mighty, Being the Hero Stories of Celtic Britain Retold from the Mabinogion*. Macmillan.

Curtin, Jeremiah. *The Fairy Tales of Eastern Europe*. McBride.

De la Mare, Walter. *The Three Mulla-Mulgars*. Knopf.

—— *Told Again*. Knopf.

Deutsch, Babette. *Heroes of the Kalevala, Finland's Saga*. Messner.

Finger, Charles J. *Tales from Silver Lands*. Doubleday, Doran.

Grierson, Elizabeth W. *The Scottish Fairy Book*. Stokes.

Grimm, The Brothers. *Fairy Tales*. Any good edition.

Hare, Christopher. *Bayard the Good Knight without Fear and without Reproach*. Dutton.

Harris, Joel Chandler. *Uncle Remus, His Songs and Sayings*. Appleton-Century.

Housman, Laurence. *Stories from the Arabian Nights* Doubleday, Doran.

Hutchinson, W. M. L. *The Golden Porch: A Book of Greek Fairy Tales.* Longmans, Green.

Jacobs, Joseph W. *English Fairy Tales.* Putnam.

Jewett, Eleanore Myers. *Egyptian Tales of Magic.* Little, Brown.

Kennedy, Howard Angus. *The New World Fairy Book.* Dutton.

Kingsley, Charles. *The Water Babies.* Dodd, Mead.

Lagerlöf, Selma. *The Wonderful Adventures of Nils.* Doubleday.

Mabie, Hamilton Wright. *Norse Stories Retold from the Eddas.* Dodd, Mead.

MacDonald, George. *At the Back of the North Wind.* Macmillan.

———— *The Princess and Curdie.* Macmillan.

———— *The Princess and the Goblin.* Macmillan.

MacKenzie, Donald A. *Wonder Tales of the East.* Blackie.

Marshall, H. E. *Stories of Beowulf.* Dutton.

Martens, Frederick W. *The Swedish Fairy Book.* Stokes.

McCormick, Dell J. *Paul Bunyan Swings His Axe.* Caxton Press.

———— *Tall Timber Tales* Caxton Press.

Olcott, Frances Jenkins, Ed. *The Book of Elves and Fairies.* Houghton Mifflin.

Ozaki, Yei Theodora, Comp. *The Japanese Fairy Book.* Dutton.

Pyle, Howard. *The Merry Adventures of Robin Hood of Great Renown in Nottinghamshire.* Scribner.

Ransome, Arthur. *Old Peter's Russian Tales.* Nelson.

Ryder, Arthur W. *Gold's Gloom: Tales from the Panchatantra.* University of Chicago Press.

Shedlock, Maria. *Eastern Stories and Legends.* Dutton.

Smith, Ruth, Ed. *The Tree of Life—Selections from the Literature of the World's Religions.* Viking Press.

Topelius, Zacharias. *Canute Whistlewinks and Other Stories.* Longmans, Green.

Wiggin, Kate Douglas and Smith, Nora Archibald. *Tales of Laughter.* Doubleday, Doran.